Praise for *Know. Own. Change.*

In the foreword of this compelling book, speaking to the racial tension and division in our country, my mentor and friend John Perkins observes, "There is no way forward without linking arms and mingling our prayers to the God of heaven to heal our land." Truer words have never been spoken. And that's the message of this book. *Know. Own. Change.* is both the title and hope-filled outline of this timely and very important resource. My dear friends Josh Clemons and Hazen Stevens write with an irresistible authenticity and honesty. Further, they show us *how* we can become portraits to a watching and waiting world of the transforming, reconciling power of the gospel. Thank you Josh and Hazen for this gift!
CRAWFORD W. LORITTS JR., author, speaker, radio host, founder and president of Beyond Our Generation

Josh Clemons and Hazen Stevens are doing the much-needed work of raising awareness and understanding around racial reconciliation, especially within the church. If we are going to see restoration around racial division, it's going to take individuals and leaders getting into action and rebuilding what we did not tear down, but what we have been called by God to put back together. This book is a necessary tool for all of us to acknowledge and accept ownership so that we can live out God's divine plan for reconciliation.
MICHAEL TODD, lead pastor of Transformation Church and bestselling author of *Relationship Goals* and *Crazy Faith*

Josh and Hazen have created a godly blueprint for coming to a place of understanding and racial reconciliation. They model this process in their own lives, so its authenticity is felt. This book is tastefully written and is an answer to a huge issue in our culture."
DALE C. BRONNER, author, founder, senior pastor, Word of Faith Family Worship Cathedral, Austell, GA

I, along with my husband "MO," met Josh and Hazen at a OneRace event in 2018. We quickly became comrades in what have been multi-episodic combines of racial reconciliation and justice throughout Atlanta. Whether it be on a stage with tens of thousands at Stone Mountain Park or a street corner in front of Centennial Olympic Park, I've watched and worked with these two zero to real quick, modern day, Jordan 1 wearing prophetic soldiers who live out what they write about. They aren't just calling for change, daily, they allow the work of racial reconciliation to challenge, change, and refresh them and all who are running alongside them.

KENDRA A. MOMON, Associate Provost, Oglethorpe University

Know. Own. Change. provides the American church with exactly what we need in this moment—a gospel-centered, challenging, and practical guide to racial reconciliation. If you and your church are serious about addressing the racial divide, you need this book.

JUSTIN E. GIBONEY, president and founder, AND Campaign; author, *Conviction and Compassion*

Josh and Hazen offer the church a grand invitation: to reconcile a racially broken world through the work and love of Jesus. If we are to be racial reconcilers, we must know, own, and engage the issues of race today through a biblical lens. This book encourages us to get back up and keep pursuing God's vision for a united and redeemed kingdom.

MICHELLE AMI REYES, Vice President, Asian American Christian Collaborative; Scholar in Residence, Hope Community Church; author, *Becoming All Things*

Jesus was a liberator, peacemaker, and reconciler, and the book *Know. Own. Change.* invites us to reflect that same hope in a world that desperately needs all three.

TERENCE LESTER, founder of Love Beyond Walls; author of *When We Stand: The Power of Seeking Justice Together* and *I See You: Opening Our Eyes to Invisible People*

Know. Own. Change. is the outcome of two men who have walked the journey of reconciliation together. It's the story of what can happen when young leaders offer their lives to see the historic pain of racism repented of, forgiven, and healed. I have known Josh Clemons and Hazen Stevens personally for many years and have had the honor of working alongside them in the ministry of reconciliation. What they offer in *Know. Own. Change.* isn't philosophy without practical experience, it's tested truth that was born out through literally hundreds of hours of prayer and thousands of hours of labor. I encourage you to open your heart and receive the truths in this book. In an hour when negativity clouds the atmosphere around the critical conversation of race, Josh and Hazen have offered us a light of hope and truth that will impact and change many.

BILLY HUMPHERY, Lead Pastor, Gate City Church; director of Gate City Missions Base

When it comes to the area of race, the church desperately needs reconcilers. I believe my two good friends Josh Clemons and Hazen Stevens are called by God to build bridges across racial lines for such a time as this. In their new book, *Know. Own. Change.*, they deal with the subject of race not only from a biblical standpoint, but from the life of two men who are living out what true racial reconciliation looks like. I am so excited about how this book is going to change lives!

LEE ALLEN JENKINS, Senior Pastor, Eagles Nest Church

Josh and Hazen are credible witnesses of God's work of bringing healing and hope to the racial tensions in America. Their love for God through the ministry of OneRace is what the church needs for times like these.

NICOLE MARTIN, author, speaker, and Senior Vice President of Ministry Impact at the American Bible Society

When it comes to racial unity movements, there is often much talk but little action. However, in this case, Josh Clemons and Hazen Stephens are the real deal. I've prayed and labored with these men. I've fasted and strategized with them. Their hearts are pure and their spirits are bold. There is so much division today, even in God's church. Yet Jesus prayed we would be one and then declared our oneness would determine our witness to this divided world. Lean in as you read the following pages— to know, own, and then change this story may be the most important work of our generation.

JOHNSON BOWIE, Senior Pastor, Victory Church, Atlanta, GA

The arc of the biblical narrative bends toward reconciliation . . . not only of individuals to their Creator through faith in Jesus Christ but to one another, then, beyond the distinctions of this world otherwise divide. Through their individual stories, collective experience, research, and practice, Josh and Hazen herein provide a constructive plan and hopeful path forward for all those interested in getting beyond accusatory rhetoric to actionable results, for the sake of the gospel and the glory of God, on earth as it is in heaven.

MARK DEYMAZ, founding pastor, Mosaic Church of Central Arkansas; cofounder and CEO, Mosaix Global Network; author, *Building a Healthy Multi-Ethnic Church* and *Disruption: Repurposing the Church to Redeem the Community*

The church has a lot to learn as it enters the race space. Followers of Jesus cannot ignore biblical reconciliation and justice if they truly desire to see God's will on earth as it is in heaven. *Know. Own. Change.* will not only reveal one's own blurred color vision, but it will challenge you to start where you are and follow the path on which the Father desires all His children to walk: healing, wholeness, transformation!

FOLEY BEACH, Archbishop and Primate of the Anglican Church in North America

KNOW

OWN

CHANGE

Journeying Toward God's
Heart for Reconciliation

JOSH CLEMONS & HAZEN STEVENS

MOODY PUBLISHERS
CHICAGO

Edited by Ginger Kolbaba
Interior design: Brandi Davis
Cover design: Charles Brock
Cover photo courtesy of OneRace Movement
Author photo for Joshua Clemons: Lakisha Clemons
Author photo for Hazen Stevens: Caleb Maglott, Compass Films

All websites and phone numbers listed herein are accurate at the time of publication but may change in the future or cease to exist. The listing of website references and resources does not imply publisher endorsement of the site's entire contents. Groups and organizations are listed for informational purposes, and listing does not imply publisher endorsement of their activities.

ISBN: 978-0-8024-2489-1

Originally delivered by fleets of horse-drawn wagons, the affordable paperbacks from D. L. Moody's publishing house resourced the church and served everyday people. Now, after more than 125 years of publishing and ministry, Moody Publishers' mission remains the same—even if our delivery systems have changed a bit. For more information on other books (and resources) created from a biblical perspective, go to www .moodypublishers.com or write to:

Moody Publishers
820 N. LaSalle Boulevard
Chicago, IL 60610

1 3 5 7 9 10 8 6 4 2

Printed in the United States of America

FROM JOSH: Lakisha, you are my dream come true. There is no one else I would want to take this journey with. Thank you for supporting, holding space, praying, correcting, pushing, and encouraging me. It is through our relationship that "cruciform love" is being perfected in me. I am forever indebted to you.

FROM HAZEN: Hannah, you are God's greatest gift to me. Your beauty, creativity, comforting presence, extraordinary wisdom, devotion in prayer, and unconditional love fill my life with goodness. There is no greater joy than to sojourn through life with you by my side. I am eternally grateful that "you are mine, and I am yours." I love you deeply.

FROM BOTH: To the pastors and city leaders of Atlanta, whose support, frequent encouragement, godly conflict, and willingness to share joys and sorrows give weight to such a work. Together, we can and will change the story.

Contents

Foreword

BY JOHN M. PERKINS

My son Spencer was so very passionate about the cause of biblical reconciliation and justice. He didn't just talk it, he lived it, forming Reconcilers Fellowship, which was a model of how Blacks and Whites could live together in unity. His example motivated me to take up the mantle and work with others who were committed to our Lord's call for unity. He would surely be on the forefront of the reconciliation movement today if he were still alive.

When I see what Joshua and Hazen are doing with OneRace Movement, it reminds me of Spencer's work, and it gives me hope for what the future holds for our nation. There is no way forward without linking arms and mingling our prayers to the God of heaven to heal our land. This is not a Black issue. And it is not a White issue. This is a sin issue. It is a sin that has festered and spoiled our witness and our voice in the presence of a watching world that wonders at the impotence of our faith.

When Joshua and Hazen asked me to come to the OneRace event at Stone Mountain, Georgia, in 2018, I was overjoyed to see more than twenty thousand young people who had come together to say, "Enough is enough." They were serious about the need to bridge the gap between Black, Brown, and White and to move forward together as an army for the Lord. Oh, how my heart was gladdened to pray over them and ask God to bless the work of their hands.

Since then, change has come in many places around our country. Even on Stone Mountain. The Stone Mountain Memorial Association recently agreed to create a museum exhibit to acknowledge the site's connection to the Ku Klux Klan. This move may have been made in part as a response to those thousands of young people who prayed on that mountain for God's justice to rain down. Little by little those old markers are coming down and people's eyes are opening to the truth of our history and the legacy it has left even until today.

When we stepped from the top of the mountain, I was able to share with the youth leaders and encourage them. I reminded them that God's call is a deeper call. It's a call for a lifetime that makes us leave everything else behind to run after it. It marks who we are. It sets the boundaries for our lives. Nothing could make me prouder than seeing how Joshua and Hazen have taken up the mantle for reconciliation and are running with all they have to win this worthy fight.

Know. Own. Change. is a powerful message I pray God will use to chip away at the strongholds that have held us captive. I agree with them that "when we sign up for reconciliation work, we sign up for the beautiful, complex, and redemptive work of bridge building. Our story of redemption is wondrous and complete because Jesus paid the high price to secure us back to God." There is hope because of Jesus' sacrifice on Calvary that reconciled us first to God and then to each other.

It is one of God's tenderest mercies to allow me to see these new leaders who are passionate and committed to the cause of biblical reconciliation. In the words of the apostle Paul, "I am already being poured out like a drink offering, and the time for my departure is near" (2 Tim. 4:6 NIV). In a sense the baton has already been passed. The cause that inspired Martin Luther King, Jr., John Lewis, Harriet Tubman, Sojourner Truth, Harriet Beecher Stowe, and so many others will live on through these young soldiers. As the writer of Hebrews encourages us:

> Since we are surrounded by such a great cloud of witnesses, let us throw off everything that hinders and the sin that so easily entangles. And let us run with perseverance the race marked out for us, fixing our eyes on Jesus, the pioneer and perfecter of faith. For the joy set before him he endured the cross, scorning its shame, and sat down at the right hand of the throne of God. Consider him who endured such opposition from sinners, so that you will not grow weary and lose heart. (Heb. 12:1–3 NIV)

Joshua Clemons and Hazen Stevens, run your race! Run your race well.

INTRODUCTION

Answering the Call

We've got to raise the conversation on reconciliation
in the church back to the common language of love.
—DR. JOHN PERKINS

L eadership is a calling."

We sat facing Dr. John Perkins, a spiritual father to the reconciliation movement in America for the past seventy years, and listened to him pour out wisdom over our lives. He had invited us to his home in Jackson, Mississippi, and we relished the privilege to sit at the feet of such a hero in the faith. While his statement held truth, its profoundness came more out of the substance and consistency of the man who spoke it.

Throughout his work, Dr. Perkins has suffered greatly for what he believes in—he carries a deep and abiding burden to see reconciliation come to the church. For that belief, he's been slandered and falsely accused, beaten within an inch of his life, and arrested and jailed unjustly on multiple occasions. Yet he has persevered.

So when he shared that wisdom, we knew we needed to heed it. He meant that leadership is not derived primarily from gifting, human ingenuity, or even the desire to right a wrong, but that true Christian leadership in any area is God-given. It is an entrustment from heaven; one we must respond to with faithfulness. And as we seek to serve the church through the ministry of reconciliation, we seek to be faithful to that calling God has put on our lives. We call men and women to be reconciled to God and to one another, and to be united as one people in devoted love to the God whose image we all bear.

> Leadership *is* a calling—not only to raise awareness and to educate, to challenge and motivate, to guide, but also to be part of the solution.

Dr. Perkins felt that call and diligently pursued it throughout his ministry. We have felt that call and have pursued it, in particular, through our OneRace Movement initiative. And because you have picked up this book, we know you have felt that call too. You sense that longing in your heart to be a reconciler in your sphere of influence. Whether in business, government, education, entertainment, or ministry, your heart burns to see racism torn down and for us to be united as one.

Leadership *is* a calling—not only to raise awareness and to educate, to challenge and motivate, to guide, but also to be part of the solution. Oftentimes, that calling will come when you least expect it. We know it did for us.

THE BIRTH OF A MOVEMENT

I (Hazen) grew up in the heart of the most affluent neighborhood in Atlanta. Though I never heard a racist slur or joke in my home growing up, and my family didn't overtly express negative views about people of color, I also never saw them engage in any peer relationships that reflected any form of racial diversity. When I was growing up, my interactions with people of color consisted mostly of those who worked for my family, not neighbors, classmates, or coworkers.

The big gleaming white-steepled church I attended from elementary to middle school did not have a single family of color. If they were there, I don't remember any Black or Brown people joining us on our summer choir tour to Yellowstone or our spring break ski trips to Colorado. They weren't part of the annual handbell choir recital or the Dutch clogging in the Christmas pageant.

Not until I went to college did I begin to understand what I'd missed because of this cultural and class homogeneity. As my eyes opened to the richness of life spent among diverse people, I lamented the absence of people of color in my life for so long. Soon I felt God calling me into the ministry of reconciliation.

Part of that ministry came when I met Josh in 2015. He was a church mobilization director for an evangelistic outreach organization, and I was serving under him as a volunteer prayer coordinator. The church where I serve as an executive pastor is well known for prayer in our city, so the organization's leaders invited me to be a member of their steering committee. Josh and I became fast friends. Josh guided me in understanding parts of the body of Christ, namely the African American church, that I had mostly grown up distant from. Through this first season of serving together, God used those experiences to show me the need for greater unity and reconciliation in the church as a whole and in our city. So a year later in 2016, when God planted an idea within several leaders to begin an initiative that would teach cities to love across color, class, and culture, I knew exactly who to call.

When Hazen approached me (Josh) about starting a reconciliation movement, I was surprised. Not because I wasn't interested but because I was preparing to plant a church in the Atlanta area. As I prayed about it and discussed it with my wife, I felt God calling me to plant in a different way and I agreed to partner with Hazen in this new ministry. We knew that if we were going to share with others how to pursue kingdom diversity and gospel-centered reconciliation, we had to intentionally practice it ourselves. And so with all vulnerability and trust on the table, we have wrestled, wept, prayed, rejoiced, and journeyed together on race. That commitment has reaped a deep friendship, stronger devotion to Jesus, and a greater outpouring for the work of reconciliation.

Together, since 2016, we have helped lead a reconciliation initiative called OneRace Movement. We have gathered more than 150,000 people in live events to stand for unity and to decry racism in every form. We have traveled more miles together, had more disagreements, and engaged in more race conversations than I could ever recall. We have listened to leaders share their stories of deep pain and wounding. And we've borne witness to stories of healing, forgiveness, and redemption. And with each celebration, we know we have more work to do, more lives to touch with the Good News of the gospel that brings about true and lasting reconciliation.

WHY RECONCILIATION IS STILL SO NEEDED

Reconciliation work is tough. It's disruptive and it is certainly complex. And yet when we sign up for it, we sign up for the beautiful and redemptive work of bridge building. When we decide to join the story of God, we become co-laborers with the great Reconciler Himself, Jesus Christ.

From the foundations of the world, God predestined Jesus to come and rescue humanity from the consequences of the fall. Through the condescension, Jesus put on flesh and dwelled among broken humanity. As He endured the cross and all of its shame, Jesus reconciled us to God and invited us to be reconciled to family.

Our story of redemption is wondrous and complete because Jesus paid the high price to secure us back to God and to make us part of His family. We are made one across lines of color, class, culture, and gender. And though we are continually becoming more like Jesus, we the church have a story that includes struggle, pain, heartache, loss, and devastation.

This is where we—the American church specifically—find ourselves. We have pain, riffs, and a sordid history relationally. We have never been one. We have never lived as a family. In fact, for a long period, part of the family was considered subhuman, reduced to property, and subjected to the unimaginable. Another part of the family, our indigenous brothers and sisters, have been robbed and conquered because of the belief that God desired this land—Manifest Destiny—for America, meaning we laid claim to it and did awful things to ensure it would be ours alone. The devastation against these members of the family has diminished the church's ability to flourish. It could

> Reconciliation work is not a one and done—because sin continues to plague us and threaten the strength and unity of the church. That's why reconciliation work is tough but necessary.

take several volumes to discuss women, the plight of our Hispanic siblings, or the Asian side of the family, and we see a common narrative unfold there as well.

To make matters worse, imagine not talking about this pain. Not lamenting it together. Not acknowledging or rectifying it, allowing the ripple effects to continue into the present.

While we stand on the shoulders of giants like Dr. Perkins and countless others, who felt God's call to reconciliation and pursued it, paying a significant price that we might enjoy the progress and the potential for equality in the present, we recognize that we too have a role to play and work to do.

Reconciliation work is not a one and done—because sin continues to plague us and threaten the strength and unity of the church. That's why reconciliation work is tough but necessary. It is necessary because we still have unaddressed wounding. It is necessary because the church, who should be leading the charge, has been derelict in its responsibility for centuries.

A GRAND INVITATION

We find ourselves in the middle of a family tragedy. But redemption is near! This is where you and I come in. This is where the church has a grand invitation. We have an opportunity to heal this broken family through the redemptive work of Jesus. We are invited to shoulder our crosses, to love sacrificially, and to fight for one another. We are invited to be *reconcilers*.

As we accept this invitation, we first need to understand the issue and the goals. So let's affirm the places we agree and work from that place of unity:

Recognize We Have a Problem

Since you're reading this book, you likely feel the racial tension in your church, community, or across America. You sense that we have a problem. However, this problem runs deeper than division, racism, and ethnocentrism. It's a problem that dates back to its inception at the fall. When Adam and Eve chose to oppose God, sin was introduced into the world. Racism at its core is sin. It is a manifestation of humankind opposing God, exalting our ideas and desires over His.

Understand That the Gospel Is the Solution

The life, death, and resurrection of Jesus provides us with a fresh start. It's through reconciliation with God that the sin problem finds resolution. It is also through the cross of Christ that we find a bridge back to a united family. Apart from the gospel we could never fully actualize this new humanity we have been called to.

Remember That Reconciliation Is the Goal

Jesus has secured a means for us to become a new humanity, a family, a holy temple, the bride of Christ. As believers, we are charged to live into this reality on the earth.

Know That We Have a Part to Play

We are invited to love God and to love one another. If we are to be fully devoted to God, then we must also be fully devoted to what He cares about: people. We must be concerned with loving our neighbors—more specifically, our diverse neighbors. The neighbors who are different from us. When we neglect that calling, we participate in the denigration of the *imago Dei* (the image of God) in them. And when we choose to love only those "like" us, we denigrate the imago Dei by overexalting it in others. These are the ways we have created the deep and historic divisions in our society. It will only be by holding a correct view of the imago Dei, one where we rightly value *all* as equally fashioned in the image of God that we will heal these divisions. This is our grand invitation.

POINTS OF FRICTION

To be sure, throughout the pages of this book, as we discuss race, history, and the gospel, we will encounter points of friction and disagreements. That friction can tempt some of us to withdraw, discredit, revise history, and reduce the gospel mandate to live reconciled. That friction can tempt others of us to overamplify the trauma of racism and filter all things through that trauma. We must be aware of both temptations. We must engage this work with a zeal for truth, and must view our shared history from a position of humility as we cleave to our common goal, which is reconciliation.

So we can be more aware, here are a few places on this journey that might cause us to do some wrestling:

- **History.** Our burden is not to present an exhaustive historical account of race, America, and the church. We aim rather to employ history to build a narrative around racial difference. We will use history to understand where we've been and how that impacts where we are. Some of the history we present may be new or have certain aspects that you've never considered. That's okay. We ask that you press through it, wrestle with the discomfort, and take breaks along the way. The only way forward is through.
- **Guilt and Shame.** For White reconcilers, it can feel as if guilt or shame are being forced upon you because of the realities of history and the candid nature with which we discuss race.

Don't disengage. It's like a muscle that is out of shape; it can be painful or exhausting to use it. It's the same with race. For many White people, conversations on race can be taboo, unfamiliar, or nonexistent. Give yourself permission to lean in, learn, lament, and become an advocate for reconciliation. Together, we are going to become "color brave," meaning we are going to learn to have honest conversations about race.

- **Racial Trauma.** For people of color (POC), the trauma of racism and history can be tough to deal with. Take your time. Our aim is to present language and a greater understanding of where we are racially. Many assume that POC know all there is to know about race and reconciliation. That simply isn't true. Give yourself permission to lean in, learn, lament, forgive, heal, and also become an advocate for reconciliation.

The work of reconciliation is a clear directive from the Scriptures. Paul said it this way: "There is neither Jew nor Greek, there is neither slave nor free, there is no male and female, for you are all one in Christ Jesus" (Gal. 3:28). We all are invited to the table of brother- and sisterhood to pursue oneness.

This pursuit will undoubtedly be tough. If you're doing it right, you will experience tense moments. You might even want to throw in the towel and give up. Don't. The body of Christ needs you. We are being knit together to tell the story of His love and grace. We are in this together. You are essential to the work.

JOURNEY TOWARD BECOMING A RECONCILER

Our hope for you as you read this book is that you'll begin the inner work of transformation to become someone who loves sacrificially and works intentionally to undermine racism in all of its forms. We call this being a *reconciler*. Reconcilers are committed to the gospel and to being a bridge across people groups. They make conscious efforts to engage with the history of race and its painful impact, and they remain committed to bringing love and healing to the world around them.

To help you on this journey, we have structured the book into four parts. In the first two chapters, we articulate the problem and tension we all feel. This is where we offer you the opportunity to move forward in your journey of transformation. For any true transformation to take place, you must first *know* the story. So in chapters 3, 4, and 5, we focus on what to know and how to know it. We will seek to answer the question, "How did we get here?" Once you know the story, you humbly can *own* the story. Chapters 6, 7, and 8 focus on what owning looks like. Here we deal with the importance of lament, confession, repentance, cultural identity, forgiveness, and practicing our faith differently. In the final chapters, 9 and 10, we spend time walking through the ways we can *change* the story.

God is inviting us to be co-laborers with Him in reconciliation, and we have immensely important work that can change the narrative for generations to come. God is asking us to respond to the invitation by being faithful to the calling. We are in this together. One family. United. For the glory of God.

1

On Earth as It Is in Heaven

We sat across from a young African American man who served as the associate pastor of a church we were inviting to join OneRace Movement. He was there to vet our sincerity and wasn't shy to challenge us. He wanted to know if we were serious about seeing through the hard work we were proposing. At one point in the conversation, with intensity, he pointed his finger at me (Hazen) and asked, "When this racial reconciliation work gets hard and messy, you will have the luxury of walking away. But"—he pointed at Josh—"he won't, because what is a choice for you is what we live with daily. So what are you going to do when the work gets hard?"

The question hung in the air as he stared at me. In that tense moment, the answer that came to me is one I have clung to ever since. His strong but appropriate challenge presented me the gift of giving voice to a conviction I held but had never expressed.

"You're right," I told him. "My being White does afford me the privilege to quit when this work gets hard. But being a disciple of Jesus demands I deny myself to follow Him. So I won't quit, because I am committed to obey."

As believers, living in allegiance to Jesus is the highest purpose. So we strive to fulfill Jesus' prayer in John 17: "that [we] may be one" (v. 11). As Jesus taught His disciples to pray, He made the desire of the Father's heart known: May "your kingdom come, your will be done, on earth as it is in heaven" (Matt. 6:10).

> Diversity is not a result of the fall. Rather, it is the desire of God's heart.

Ultimately, we do this reconciliation work because Jesus is worthy of a beautiful bride, adorned in holiness, whose worship is rapturous and whose love is evident.

We received a foretaste of that glory, of what the church was designed to be, when OneRace brought together a solemn assembly at the nation's largest Confederate monument in August 2018. That day five hundred pastors and twenty-five thousand believers gathered at Stone Mountain of Georgia on the fifty-fifth anniversary of Dr. Martin Luther King, Jr.'s "I Have a Dream" speech. We met together to renounce racism and to call for reconciliation. We prayed to see the stronghold of racism broken over America and for the church to be reconciled. We rallied around the cross of Christ to lament, repent, heal, and worship.

As I (Josh) stared out into the crowd and witnessed the beautiful mosaic of diversity, two things hit me acutely.

First, the sound of prayer, worship, lament, and repentance overwhelmed me. This moment represented redemption; it was a token of a glory in the age to come. "This is what You want," I prayed. "A bride pursuing unity together." It was a picture of Revelation 7 reality:

After this I looked, and behold, a great multitude that no one could number, from every nation, from all tribes and peoples and languages, standing before the throne and before the Lamb, clothed in white robes, with palm branches in their hands, and crying out with a loud voice, "Salvation belongs to our God who sits on the throne, and to the Lamb!" (vv. 9–10)

This throne room scene shows us that diversity is not a result of the fall. Rather, it is the desire of God's heart. Multiethnic worship and multiethnic beauty surrounding the throne of God communicate the importance that God places on diverse expression. But it doesn't stop there. The innumerable multitude is unified in its worship. Though different languages, rhythms, and cadences are being sung, the worship experience is unified nonetheless. This is what God desires here and now—a bride composed of uniqueness, diversity, and beauty all standing in unity.

The second thing that hit me was that we still have so much work to do! This gathering was but a moment that paled in comparison to the centuries of racial terror, oppression, and trauma so many people had experienced. We must never underestimate the stronghold of racism. It has been fortified by centuries of transgressions, right up to the present day.

What exactly is racism? We define racism as the sin of having power over another resulting in partiality that impedes the flourishing of individuals and ethnic groups. This sin can be committed through intentional and passive actions. It is evinced on both an individualized and structural basis, affecting individuals and the systems of society.

Individualized racism occurs between individuals. It might be as subtle as an unconscious bias that is held about a person or a group. Or perhaps it could be as overt as outright hatred for a person or people group. Whatever the case, our held beliefs about a person or persons, whether conscious or unconscious, informs our actions toward them. This is as subtle as a passing thought or an unconscious action, such as clutching one's purse while on an elevator with a person of color or the assumption that persons of Hispanic heritage can't speak English. The extreme of individualized overt racism is prejudice that hinders the flourishing or diminishes the imago Dei in an individual. An example would be the Charleston church massacre in 2015 that cost nine individuals their lives.

Many have pursued the work against racism and for reconciliation—heroes such as Sojourner Truth, Harriet Beecher Stowe, Frederick Douglass, Dr. John Perkins, Dr. Brenda Salter McNeil, Dr. Michael Emerson, and countless others. Many quietly engage in reconciliation in their neighborhoods and communities, known only to God. And we can see the results of their labors of love.

But just because we have come so far doesn't mean we rest on the laurels of others' hard work. We still have work to do. God is calling us to engage in that work.

To be sure, we put in work. We practice relationship building, repentance, forgiveness, prayer, and even justice pursuits. Yet lasting reconciliation isn't established through any single efforts. Reconciliation is the convergence of all of these things, sustained over time, in a spirit of sacrificial love for neighbor. We join the work of God and advance the cause of horizontal reconciliation in our city and across our nation. We live to see God's kingdom and will done on earth as it is in heaven.

That's why gathering at Stone Mountain that day to take back what the sin of racism has stolen from us was so important. We gathered to know, own, and change the story. Because there can be no reconciliation without first a great reckoning.

THE REBIRTH OF THE KU KLUX KLAN

Engraved into the side of Stone Mountain are Generals Robert E. Lee, Stonewall Jackson, and Jefferson Davis—a massive shrine dedicated to the Confederacy. These men were professed "Christians."[1] Yet all were slave owners and battled to maintain this atrocity.

But Stone Mountain is more than an engraved monument. It represents a dark hour for the church. On Thanksgiving night in 1915, William Joseph Simmons, a Methodist Episcopal minister, led a group of fifteen men to the top of Stone Mountain. There they built an altar and placed a Bible and an American flag on it. Then they erected a sixteen-foot-tall cross and set it ablaze. Just weeks earlier this same group gathered to lynch Leo Frank, an innocent Jewish man.[2]

After watching one of the first feature-length films, *Birth of a Nation*, Simmons was inspired to fan the flames of the KKK, which had physically disbanded in the 1870s when Jim Crow laws secured white supremacy throughout the country.[3] The film, also viewed at the White House by then-president Woodrow Wilson, presents racial terrorism as a means to preserve the American way of life through domination, intimidation, and violence against primarily Black people. Notorious for menacing and terrorizing people of color, Catholics, and Jews, the KKK, explains historian Jemar Tisby, "crafted a vision of a white America and, more specifically, a white Christian America."[4]

Let us not be quick to rush past the fact that Rev. Simmons led the way in the rebirth of the KKK. These men who stood with him were "Christians" who lynched Frank. And their actions led to the lynching of countless others. As historian Kelly Baker notes in *The Gospel According to the Klan*, "The Klan [of the early twentieth century] was not just an order to defend America but also a campaign to protect and celebrate Protestantism. It was a *religious* order."[5]

It is stories like this one that begs the question, where was the church as a whole in response? Where was the institution that is supposed to preach brotherhood and make it a reality in its body? Where was the credible representation of Christ to a watching world?

To be sure, there were advocates of racial justice, working to fight against this kind of sin. However, it takes the complicity of the majority to produce such a catastrophic narrative.

This is the problem with American church history. The prophetic voice of the church has been largely silent. We have been complicit and absent. We have lagged in places in which we should have been leading. We have been negligent regarding things that offend God, and that harm brothers and sisters of color. Sadly, throughout American history, the church corporately and Christians individually have often participated in championing violence and evil, living antithetical to our calling.

RACISM THAT LINGERS INTO THE PRESENT

In the fall of 2013, I (Josh) was living in Dallas, Texas, while working on my Masters of Divinity in Tulsa, Oklahoma. I had to commute weekly through several small towns to get to classes. On one occasion, a police officer in one of those towns pulled me over. Thinking that perhaps I'd unintentionally been caught speeding, I readied myself to present my license and car registration. What I didn't expect, however, was the officer to greet me by telling me to get out of my car. Without another word or explanation, he escorted me to the back of the police car. Based on his actions and demeanor, I got this feeling that if I were to resist or inquire or even act in any way that may indicate a failure to comply, I could surely lose my life.

Within moments another officer arrived and began questioning me. "You're from Texas?"

"Yes, sir."

"What are you doing here?"

I answered each question, though I was still unsure why I was being questioned or what I had supposedly done.

After being held on the side of the road in the back of that police car for an hour, I finally was told, "You fit the description of someone we've been looking for. But you are free to go."

Sigh of relief. No ticket. No arrest.

I would write this off as a fluke, but the same thing happened twice in the same town. Was it just that my black skin was the target?

This, or much worse, is the experience of many people of color. Whether it's overt, covert, or systemic racism, it wounds us just the same. It prohibits people from flourishing.

The reality is that we live between two Americas, or as sociologist and civil rights activist W. E. B. Du Bois put it, we exist with a "double consciousness":

> It is a peculiar sensation, this double-consciousness, this sense of always looking at one's self through the eyes of others, of measuring one's soul by the tape of a world that looks on in amused contempt and pity. One ever feels his two-ness—an American, a Negro; two souls, two thoughts, two unreconciled strivings; two warring ideals in one dark body, whose dogged strength alone keeps it from being torn asunder.[6]

I know this pain all too well. The trauma of *otherness* is indescribable and can be understood only by those who have traveled the way.

To be sure, racism isn't merely individualistic and white supremacy isn't relegated to hoods, robes, and burning crosses. No, it's bigger than that. The dark past is, too, a dark present. It impacts the lives of millions of people of color. We call this *systemic racism*. It is the ingraining of racism culturally that informs laws and impacts peoples of color's ability to flourish.

Systemic racism occurs in the systems of society that accommodate one group while disadvantaging another. This can be overt or covert. Some examples of overt systemic racism include the stop-and-frisk laws that targeted ethnic minorities, Jim Crow policies that relegated Blacks to an inferior status in society, and red lining that restricted homeownership by Black people to particular areas.

Though no longer "legal," their effects linger. Consider the ways this systemic racism continues to impact people of color:

Wealth[7]

- On average White families have $188,200 of accumulated wealth.
- On average Black families have $36,100 of accumulated wealth.
- On average Hispanic families have $24,100 of accumulated wealth.

Poverty[8]

- 10.1 percent of White people live in poverty. Approximately 21.3 million people.
- 20.8 percent of Black people live in poverty. Approximately 8.3 million people.
- 17.6 percent of Hispanic people live in poverty. Approximately 9.3 million people.

Crime and Imprisonment

- Nearly 1.5 million people incarcerated as of 2018.
- 30 percent of the prison population is White (about 436,500 people)—despite the fact that White people make up 64 percent of the US population (approximately 211 million people).
- 23 percent of the prison population is Hispanic (about 336,500 people)—despite the fact that Hispanic people make up 16 percent of the US population (approximately 53 million people).
- 33 percent of the prison population is Black (about 475,900 people)—despite the fact that Black people make up 12 percent of the US population (approximately 40 million people).[9]
- Hispanic people are two times more likely to be killed by police than White people.
- Black people are three times more likely to be killed by police than White people.
- Black people have been 28 percent of those killed by police in 2020 despite being only 13 percent of the population.[10]

Employment[11]

- 3.3 percent of White people unemployed.
- 6.6 percent of Black people unemployed.
- 14 percent of White people underemployed.
- 24.9 percent of Black people underemployed.

Gender[12]

- Asian women earn $.90 on the dollar of White men.
- White women earn $.79 on the dollar of White men.

- Black women earn $.62 on the dollar of White men.
- Hispanic women earn $.54 on the dollar of White men.

This data tells us one of two things: The White race is the superior race, and all others are inferior. Or it tells us that the racial events of our past have significantly impacted our present. It could tell us that the trauma of racism in the West has diminished minorities' ability to flourish in America. The data helps us to measure the impact of systemic racism and its residual effects. And it reminds us of the work we all still need to do.

DISCIPLESHIP DEMANDS LOVING OBEDIENCE

Stepping up and into the work of reconciliation doesn't come easily. It is a journey of increasing resolve and deepening conviction that Jesus has called us to love our neighbors as ourselves. And in order to do this, we can't selectively care only for the neighbors who look like us. We can be tempted toward living in apathy because, frankly, it's easier—even in the church. We have seen many organizational boards and leadership teams that are leading multicultural businesses and ministries, but their decision-making bodies are homogeneously White and male. That leads us to ask the hard question, "Why is that?" Many of the economic, political, and social structures of our society favor the majority's preferences, and historically have systematically elevated Whites into positions of power over other races.

> If we believe what we pray when we say the Lord's Prayer—that God's kingdom come and God's will be done on earth as it is in heaven—then we have laid down our right to remain indifferent toward the plight of our neighbor.

It can be more comfortable to simply remain neutral, ignorant, or even callous and deny the challenges minorities face in America. However, if we are Christians who have given our allegiance to Jesus, if we believe what we pray when we say the Lord's Prayer— that God's kingdom come and God's will be done on earth as it is in heaven—then we have laid down our right to remain indifferent toward the plight of our neighbor. Jesus is leading His church into oneness, so we must be resolved to discern and do our part to follow Him there.

Yes, I (Hazen) follow Him as a leader in a reconciliation movement, but I also follow Him as a pastor in a local church, a neighbor, a husband, and a father. I may move in life from one assignment to another, but by God's grace I won't ever *quit*. Loving our sister or brother and living reconciled to them is not an option; it is a kingdom prerogative that He has called us to obey.

Furthermore, real love demands that my neighbors' challenges have now become my own. Scripture teaches this truth plainly. Paul wrote in Galatians 6: "*Carry each other's burdens*, and in this way you will *fulfill the law of Christ*. . . . Let us not become weary in doing good, for at the proper time we will reap a harvest if we do not give up. Therefore, as we have opportunity, *let us do good to all people*, especially to those who belong to the family of believers" (vv. 2, 9–10 NIV). This is what it means to obey the second commandment, "love your neighbor as yourself" (Mark 12:31) and to follow Christ's law: "In everything, do to others what you would have them do to you, for this sums up the Law and the Prophets" (Matt. 7:12 NIV).

GETTING CLEAR ON THE BIBLICAL
CONCEPT OF RECONCILIATION

As Hazen and I have journeyed in the race space, we have noted multiple times to each other that we have yet to find two people who would define "reconciliation" the same way. In fact, when I am at seminars, conferences, or in conversation, I often wonder what each person means by the term. I have heard everything from reconciliation being strictly about preaching the gospel to being strictly about pursuing justice and action. One thing is clear: we are unclear about the biblical concept of reconciliation.

Generally, we agree that something is fractured and in need of repair. We also agree that we, the church, play a role. Where the descent begins is: How fractured are we really? What does the gospel have to say about said fracture? And what does God require *me* to do about this prevailing problem?

Our friends with the Reimagine Group and Barna commissioned a study on varying beliefs regarding reconciliation. As we consider the above question, here are their findings:

- 94 percent of Christians believe the church plays a crucial role in the work of racial reconciliation.
- 87 percent of White Christians and 82 percent of Black Christians believe that hostility exists between the two racial groups.
- 84 percent of Black Americans state they experience social disadvantage, compared to 62 percent of White Americans who would agree that Black Americans are disadvantaged.
- 59 percent of White Christians believe racism is a problem of the past, compared to 39 percent of Black Christians who would agree with that statement.[13]

Barna's senior vice president, Brooke Hempell, speaks to this data on the sentiments of White and Black people in the church: "This dilemma demonstrates those supposedly most equipped for reconciliation do not see the need for it."[14]

There is a great dissonance between our believed theology (orthodoxy) and how we practice that theology (orthopraxy). This is a discipleship failure. We lack a clear understanding of what the gospel invites us into. Thus we have a shortsighted understanding of reconciliation work, which leads to bad outcomes. The reason we aren't experiencing reconciliation is due to our discipleship failure.

So how do we change that?

First, we need to understand that reconciliation is the process by which people across the spectrum of diversity are made right with God and each other through the power of the gospel of Jesus Christ. This process includes confession, lament, repentance, forgiveness, and restoration.

Reconciliation starts with God making the first move. As Paul explained: "God, being rich in mercy, because of the great love with which he loved us, even when we were dead in our trespasses, made us alive together with Christ—by grace you have been saved" (Eph. 2:4–5). We are then invited to move toward one another.

This is reconciliation: Jesus restores the possibility of relationship with us through His faithful and holy life, His obedience to the cross despites its shame, and His resurrection from the dead. Jesus rescues our story. But from what exactly? Sin. As a result of the fall, sin created a chasm between God and man, fracturing the relationship. Our relationship with God was once broken, in need of repair. But thanks be to God, while we were utterly helpless, Christ came at just the right time and died for us sinners. Jesus came to restore the broken relationship. He conquered sin, death, hell, and the grave, so that whoever would believe in Him might have everlasting life. Jesus is the great Reconciler.

Why start with the cross? Why start with reconciliation to God? Because if God hadn't made the first move, we could never move toward one another. We must emphatically proclaim that it is because of Jesus that we are able to be reconciled to God and to each other: "He himself is our peace, who has made us both one and has broken down in his flesh the dividing wall of hostility by abolishing the law of commandments expressed in ordinances, that he might create in himself one new man in place of the two, so making peace, and might reconcile us both to God in one body through the cross, thereby killing the hostility" (Eph. 2:14–16).

There was this underlying tension present in the relationship. Ephesians 2:11–16 captures this tension through the temple court interaction. Gentiles were only allowed in the "court of the Gentiles." They were precluded from the other courts that only Jews had access to. In fact, signs were posted that stated if Gentiles left their area, they would be killed. The wall that divided the two was referred to as "the wall of hostility." Hostile because it was a wall of ethnic division that carried with it the penalty of death. To be sure, the Gentiles believed in the God of the Jews, but because they weren't ethnic Jews, they weren't allowed into the other spaces.[15]

Paul drew on this "wall of hostility" idea in describing what Christ had done for the Jews and Gentiles, and for us. Through Christ's obedience to the cross, He secured peace between the two groups. He has destroyed the wall of hostility and made the two groups one. In fact, it goes further than that: He has created a new humanity out of the two. Because of the cross, God has reconciled the fractured relationship between the Jews and the Gentiles.[16]

So what is God's goal in reconciliation? What is the mission of Christ in horizontal reconciliation? He desires to restore wholeness to broken relationships. His desire is to move people groups from being outsiders with one another to being family: "You are no longer strangers and aliens, but you are fellow citizens with the saints and members of the household of God" (Eph. 2:19). It's wild to think that the Cross is able to take a tumultuous relationship and restore it, take a fracture and mend it, and take what's divided and unite it. But that is the power of the gospel; it causes dead things to come back to life.[17]

Because of Jesus Christ reconciliation is possible. Reconciliation is possible across colors, classes, cultures, and gender. The history of Black and White relations would be hopeless to overcome but for the blood of Jesus and the power of the Cross. He is able to unite us. But we have to sign up for the journey.

We have to desire reconciliation. We have to long for a pure and spotless bride at Jesus' return. A bride who is rid of the stain of racism and division, supremacy and unforgiveness. A friend and fellow reconciler Johnson Bowie said it to me this way, "When Christians live divided lives, we are saying to a watching world that the blood of Jesus is strong enough to save us, but not strong enough to unite us." For far too long this has been the testimony of the church. It's time for a new path forward. It is time for us to be more in love with the arduous work of reconciliation than we are with the mere idea of reconciliation. It's time for us to fight for oneness.

If we are going to move forward, we have to see each other. We have to see the wall of hostility that exists between people groups. We have to see the chasm that sin wrought. We have to see our history and cultural norms. We have to grapple with racism and the trauma that needs healing.

Here's the reality: there can be no reconciliation without a great reckoning. We must reckon with all that divides us that we might see reconciliation in our moment in history.

2

Journeying Toward Wellness

At nineteen years old, I (Josh) thought I was invincible. I had just graduated high school. I was working full time at Chick-fil-A. I had my first apartment. I secured a part-time position as a youth pastor. I planned to start college in the spring. Life was going well. So I couldn't have been more surprised when one evening at a church gathering with friends, the room began to spin.

Though I played it off as nothing serious, over the next several weeks, I grew so weak I had difficulty getting out of bed.

I lost fifteen pounds—even though I was eating and drinking more than usual. And I felt terrible.

One day my boss took me aside after my shift. "Josh, I don't think you're well. You need to see a doctor. Your behavior is different, you seem unclear in communication, you've made a dozen mistakes, and you've been late three times this week. This isn't you."

"I'm fine," I said, still trying to blow off my symptoms. "I'll do better tomorrow."

"You are not fine," she said firmly. "I'm concerned about you. Go see a doctor. We'll cover your time off."

The next day I went to see the doctor. After chatting briefly about my symptoms, he left the room and came back with a small machine. He pricked my finger, and tested my blood. After a few seconds, the machine read "HIGH."

That notice sent me directly to the hospital where I spent the day getting tests and IV fluids, and waiting for results.

Finally the doctor came in and announced, "The good news is none of your organs have been damaged. Your kidneys and liver are okay. The bad news is you have type 1 diabetes."

I wasn't even sure what that was.

"A normal range for blood glucose levels is 70 to 120 mg, or an A1C at 5.5 or below, which is the measure of your blood glucose over a three-month period. Your blood glucose is more than 1,000 and your A1C is 13.4."

I swallowed hard. This was serious.

"This disease, if left untreated, will kill you in a matter of hours or days," he continued. "And if you are not intentional in your care, it can make life really miserable for you. You have a major part to play in your care. What we do next will make all the difference."

I nodded, now feeling anything *but* invincible.

He called my mom, who immediately came to the hospital. The doctor chatted with us for what seemed like hours. He set me up with an endocrinologist, a diabetes nurse, and a nutritionist to get me adjusted to my new normal. He gave me lots of medication and a clear plan of action. He touched base with me every week for months.

Today, thirteen years later, I am healthy, and my diabetes is under control.

This experience reminds me of the church in America. We are unaware that we have a life-threatening disease. We are sick and we can't seem to get well. We are fatigued. We see the symptoms and they are virtually killing us. We need to get well.

The first step on the journey of healing is to diagnose where we are. Next, we must determine what role each of us plays. Finally, we need to chart the course and begin intentionally moving from here to "well."

DIAGNOSING WHERE WE ARE

In his 1967 best seller *Where Do We Go From Here?*, Dr. Martin Luther King, Jr. wrote, "Whites, it must frankly be said, are not putting in a similar mass effort to reeducate themselves out of their racial ignorance. It is an aspect of their sense of superiority that the white people of America believe they have so little to learn."[1]

Essentially, Dr. King directly addressed the underlying impediment to progress. We must do the same.

While "Where do we go from here?" is a good question, I believe Christians of *all* races need to ask themselves a further question: "*Why* haven't we gone from here?" To pose the question "Where do we go from here?" assumes that we know where we are. It assumes we've located ourselves on this journey and are ready to engage in action. Yet before we can answer, we need to address an underlying apathy, ignorance, and/or resistance we may be experiencing. We must locate ourselves on this journey.

> It is arrogant to engage in a space where we have limited knowledge yet insist on leading.

Locating Ourselves Includes Reeducation and Reorientation

Transformation *is* possible. Reeducation and reorientation are the keys. As Dr. King stated, we need to be reeducated out of our racial ignorance and need to be reoriented to the problem at hand. When we move from attempting to *do* something about the racial divide to first *seeing* it more clearly, we move from pride to humility. Pride says, *I know it all*; humility takes the posture of a learner ready to receive.

If we are going to live into reconciliation, we must be willing to get uncomfortable. Humility is uncomfortable. It forces us to reconsider what we know and takes the posture of a pupil. It is arrogant to engage in a space where we have limited knowledge yet insist on leading. Imagine going to a hospital in scrubs and demanding to perform surgery because you dissected a frog in your high school biology class. That would be absurd. It is just as absurd to proceed in reconciliation efforts without investing time to understand clearly the racial divide.

How do we reeducate and reorient? By wrestling with the truth. If we are going to journey toward reconciliation, we need clarity from history and the Scriptures about reconciliation. As Latasha Morrison so rightly pointed out in *Be the Bridge*:

> Historical truth plays an important role in our understanding of how we arrived in our current racial tension. Without looking back, without understanding the truth of our history, it's difficult to move forward in healthy ways. And even though it might be painful to recount our history as a country, denying it leads us nowhere. Truth is the foundation of awareness, and awareness is the first step in the process of reconciliation. Jesus said as much: "You will know the truth and the truth will make you free."[2]

We need to know the truth about ourselves and the truth about the church. A certain power comes with the truth. It allows us to see things as they are and not what we hoped or dreaded they would be. It allows us to diagnose where we really are.

Locating Ourselves Includes Rediscipling

We've found that many Christian leaders we've consulted over the years want to start with the fruit instead of the root. They want to solve their "diversity problem" as a means of doing reconciliation work. Yet in doing so they fail to see the underlying miscarriage of discipleship. They fail to locate where they are. So their solution often looks like this: they build a cross-cultural relationship, hire a diverse candidate, or hold a reconciliation prayer meeting. While these things aren't inherently bad, if they stand alone, they are devoid of the substance of real transformation.

In starting with the idea of seeking diversity, they fail to address the underlying discipleship failure that created the diversity vacuum in the first place. Focusing solely on diversity will only exacerbate and mask the underlying issue.

Following this approach makes transformation of the heart and mind inconsequential. "Doing" is prioritized; "seeing" is underappreciated. Suddenly there are people of color involved who have been negatively impacted. Though these intentions are good, their impact can be bad. Friend, we must undergo heart transformation through reeducating, reorienting, and rediscipling. We must see the racial divide clearly before engaging the doing aspect of this work.

DETERMINING OUR ROLE

At the heart of reconciliation is the Great Commission, the most explicit invitation to make disciples, and reflexively to be disciples.

Jesus told us to "go therefore and make disciples of all nations, baptizing them in the name of the Father and of the Son and of the Holy Spirit" (Matt. 28:19).

We cannot make disciples if we aren't disciples. Being a disciple, we must follow the ways and teachings of Jesus. He imparts to us a meaningful exchange that leaves an indelible mark on us. An ancient Jewish proverb best captures this idea: "Follow a Rabbi, drink in his words, and be covered with the dust of his feet."[3]

In Jewish culture disciples were to follow their rabbi so closely that the disciples would be covered in the dust that his feet would kick up. We, too, must follow Jesus this closely. There is so much more that is *caught* than *taught*—things we would miss if we keep Him at a distance. What we witness in the Gospel writings of Jesus' life and ministry, we must seek to imitate. We must seek to operate with respect to His teaching and example, deriving a kingdom ethic for engaging with the world. It is Him we preach; it is also Him we must seek to imitate. Jesus said, "I am the way, and the truth, and the life" (John 14:6). And Paul tells us: "Be imitators of me, as I am of Christ" (1 Cor. 11:1). The idea of imitation can just as easily be translated, "Follow the example." We must seek to follow the example of Jesus, that we too might be covered in His dust.

How does this discipleship affect reconciliation and justice work? Again, our role is to follow Jesus' example. We see Jesus continually moving toward the tension. He is always upsetting the status quo. Early in His ministry, Jesus encountered a woman at a well (see John 4). He didn't distance Himself from her, as was the custom. Instead Jesus interacted with her, treating her with respect and love.

He broke the cultural norm to welcome her into His kingdom. He engaged with a woman—and one with a questionable reputation. Women were culturally thought of as second-class citizens in

Greco-Roman culture. Her gender and dubious morality combined with her ethnic identity as a Samaritan—a half-Jewish, half-Gentile ethnicity—made Jesus' action quite scandalous.

Later, Jesus discussed the idea of loving our neighbor. To illustrate who our neighbor is, He told the story of a man, presumably Jewish, who was a victim of a violent crime that left him half dead on the side of the road. A Levite and a priest—two devout, religious individuals whom we would expect to stop and hope would help—ignored the man's plight. But then a Samaritan entered the scene, saw him, and immediately stepped into compassionate action.

Jesus used the "hated" and "inferior" Samaritan, someone of a different ethnicity, to demonstrate mercy, justice, and reconciliation. Not only did the Samaritan meet the man's immediate needs but followed through in the days ahead to make sure the man was on the way to full recovery.

It was as if Jesus was using the foolish things to confound the wise. The Jews were supposed to be the pious and most spiritual. Yet, they were the ones attempting to qualify or disqualify whom they must show compassion toward. Yet Jesus clearly

> Until the American church as a whole reflects the compassion, mercy, and justice of Jesus' ministry, we have not lived into reconciliation.

disrupted this idea by showing that all are welcomed to the Master's table. Jesus was rediscipling the Jews through His example and teachings. Religiosity had created a barrier for the Gentiles to come to faith. It had allowed the Jews to believe that they were superior and the Gentiles inferior. In every sense, Jesus was spotlighting their *Jewish supremacy*.

As we consider the church in America, we see that she has been actively and passively discipled by American culture. We have integrated many American ideals, and thus resemble such. The problem is that we were commanded to be conformed to the image of Christ, not to the image of culture. There is much rediscipling that must take place if the church is to emerge as reconciled. Until the American church as a whole reflects the compassion, mercy, and justice of Jesus' ministry, we have not lived into reconciliation. They ought to see it in our love, our advocacy, and our impact on the world. We must become imitators of Christ. Discipleship is the way forward. Discipleship is our clear role.

CHARTING THE COURSE TO WELLNESS

As we follow Jesus' teaching and example, we become better equipped to chart our course toward wellness. So what is the course? What is our approach to knowing, owning, and changing the story?

Humility and a gospel resolve.

Since the days of Cain and Abel, the powers of darkness have been working to turn humanity against one another with murderous intent. So it is of utmost importance that we hold fast to humility and the gospel. Humility is relinquishing my power to choose, reason away, or to disengage. Rather, choosing to stay, empathize, and seek to understand. We need humility—because this history is dark, evil by nature, and present with us. We need a gospel resolve—because it's our only hope for true reconciliation.

If you're a person of color, this course can prove difficult because your story intersects in both historical and present trauma. You may encounter racial difficulty daily from social interactions and microaggressions that constantly remind you of your otherness. It is a wound regularly aggravated and exacerbated. If you find yourself in this place, please know that you are seen, known, and welcomed to be vulnerable in the presence of those who love you and, most importantly, in the presence of Jesus. Your course to chart is to show up for the journey. The church needs you to tell the truth, with patience and grace. Your wounding and pain are real, but please don't retreat. We, the family of God, are incomplete without you. We must bow our knees, expose our hearts, lean in, and cleave to our brothers and sisters in love, humility, and compassion.

If you are part of the majority culture (White), this course can prove difficult because it can feel like an assault on your identity and personhood. The tension will be great, but you are needed. We are incomplete without you. For us to emerge as one body, you must show up in strength, humility, and courage. Together, we must learn to suffer, lament, and heal the broader body of Christ.

This transformational journey can be tough for everyone due to the depth of the wounding, and because many of the majority culture, including within the church, have been the ones wielding the proverbial knife. Truthfully, I (Hazen) can't deny as a White man that it wears on the soul to be identified continually with the group who is most responsible for the most harm. Though I haven't personally contributed, I have doubtlessly benefitted. Yet I get to play a part in rectifying these wrongs in my day, and a unique role in bringing redemption.

We can't begin to change the world around us, until we allow ourselves to be changed. Jesus' ministry model is always first incarnational, meaning we must not just *do* differently, but be renewed in heart and mind so we become the change we want to see. This has become painfully obvious to me as I have endeavored to *do* the work of reconciliation. I learned early on in this ministry that as a wealthy, educated White man, I am used to being the decision maker and often the first and last to speak on a matter. And I am ashamed to admit that too often I embraced it without thinking of the leadership abilities and insight of others different from myself. But this sinful pattern I was accustomed to needed to die in my life. I have had to let the Spirit work on this self-centered way of relating to those around me, releasing my need to control and have my way.

I need to show up with my whole heart, but not only on my terms with the precondition that I get to be in charge. The racial and class identity the world shaped in me needed to be conformed to a kingdom identity of humility and meekness. This doesn't mean I don't ever express leadership, but I must do so first and foremost as a servant. The journey toward wellness requires a mind that is hungry to listen and learn so it can *know*, an engaged heart that is willing to *own*, and hands that are willing to serve so the story can *change*.

WE MUST BECOME ONE

During one of the most critical moments of Jesus' time on earth, just before His glorification, He interceded on behalf of His disciples and the future church; He poured His heart out, expressing His great desire for His beloved. This prayer is considered the climax of Jesus' teaching and witness to the disciples. As one commentator wrote: "No attempt to describe the prayer can give a just idea of its sublimity, its pathos, its touching yet exalted character, its tone at once of tenderness and triumphant expectation."[4] Listen to the words of Jesus as He prays:

> I do not ask for these only, but also for those who will believe in me through their word, that they may all be one, just as you, Father, are in me, and I in you, that they also may be in us, so that the world may believe that you have sent me. (John 17:20–21)

We need a new way forward. This pursuit must encompass the tenderness of Jesus' and the Father's relationship. It must be built on the truth of Christ's love for us and His desire for us to be one. Jesus' request that "they may all be one" is a tall order. Jesus is undoubtedly looking down the annals of time and He sees the western church. He sees our rugged individualism. He sees our bad theology of loving neighbor and imago Dei. He sees our tumultuous history. He sees us in the present, and He still prays "that they may all be one."

Through sacrificial love and intentionality, this oneness can become a reality. And on the other side of the reconciled church is a credible witness to a watching world. Jesus continued His prayer, saying that they may be one "so that the world may believe that you have sent me." There is something about our oneness, our reconciled state that will provoke a watching world to believe and inquire about Jesus.

Gospel-centered reconciliation is incapable of failing. Jesus secured it and that settled it. If reconciliation efforts are "failing," it's because of user error. It's because of complicit, self-centered individuals, and hate is the reason.

Jesus has never failed. The sacrifice offered on Calvary is sufficient. The blood of Jesus is powerful and potent, filled with limitless reconciling abilities. God is not only reconciling people to Himself, He is reconciling all things. If we were in the Black church I (Josh) grew up in, this would be reason enough for a praise break. Yes, hallelujah! God is at work in the present racial degeneracy, working to reconcile all things back to Himself. And we get the privilege to be part of that work.

3

Know the Story of Racism in America

When I (Josh) was about twelve years of age, my mother bought a lawn mower for me and sent me on my way. For years on any given sunny day, I could be found mowing lawns.

One of my favorite customers was Bishop Otis Clark, a member of our church whom we affectionately called Dad Clark. He was in his nineties, and had until recently mowed his own lawn. Whenever he would get up to share his thoughts with the congregation on Sunday morning, he would always say, "Remember, if you're on God's side, you're on the winning side."

One day when I was sixteen, my friends and I visited him, and he told us his story. It was fascinating to hear about history through what he'd experienced. I'll never forget the look of anguish on his face, though, when he shared about losing his stepfather. He was eighteen years of age in 1921. And one day in May, he saw his stepfather at the beginning of the day, and never saw him again.

"What happened?" my friend Tony asked.

Dad Clark paused as if we should already know. Then he gathered himself and began to share about the Tulsa Race Massacre of 1921.

He told about the sound of bombs and machine guns. The smoke and the fire. The destruction and the ruins. The loss and grief. It all seemed to overwhelm this precious man's face.

I was spellbound and horrified. I had never heard this story before—and it wasn't far from where we were visiting with him.

Black Wall Street or The Greenwood District, as it is formally known, was home to one the largest Black-owned commerce centers in the nation around the turn of the twentieth century. Not long after slavery ended, African Americans seeking freedom and escaping terror in the South flocked to Oklahoma and established more than fifty communities. Tulsa became home to the wealthiest Black district in the States.

It was a bustling place of luxury hotels, doctors' offices, grocery stores, and movie theaters. It even had its own school and bus system. More than ten thousand Black residents called the Greenwood District home.

On May 30, 1921, Dick Rowland, a Black man, was riding in an elevator with a White woman named Sarah, who happened to be the elevator operator. She later accused him of sexual assault. This lie provoked a catastrophic terrorist attack—a mob of about 1,500 White people descended on Black Wall Street and burned it to the ground.

So terrible was the riot that to this day, we don't know if three hundred or three thousand people perished. In fact, eyewitnesses claimed they watched city officials dump bodies into mass graves across Tulsa.[1]

Dad Clark's stepfather became a victim—as did Dad Clark, as

he was dodging bullets and violence while seeking to save lives on that dreadful day. Dad Clark lost a parent and influential male role model that day, but he lost much more. He lost his sense of home. His expression, decades later, showed that he still bore the trauma.[2]

At sixteen years old, I didn't understand the significance of such an event. But to this day, I can't understand why I never learned about this tragedy in school. Why was such a significant story about Black prosperity, Tulsa's history, kept silent? And more important, how can we ever change the story to bring healing if we don't *know* the story?

Race and racism have shaped us in profound ways, yet we are unaware of the depth of its impact. For example, Tulsa is still racially segregated. North Tulsa continues to be home to a majority of African Americans, and by and large, this area is economically depressed. This is all connected. This is all part of a greater story.

But it isn't just Tulsa. Look at any major city and you can see the remnants of past racist decisions. Chicago, the third largest city in the United States, is also still one of the most segregated, with Blacks primarily living on the South Side, while Whites reside on the North Side.

And it isn't just residential areas that retain that segregation. The church does too. As Dr. King observed: "We must face the fact that . . . the church is still the most segregated major institution in America. At 11:00 on Sunday morning when we stand and sing and Christ has no east or west, we stand at the most segregated hour in this nation. This is tragic. Nobody of honesty can overlook this."[3]

> History is often . . . revised, idealized, and anesthetized to fit the idea of goodness, projecting the story we want told about White America.

It's heartbreaking that this segregation exists, but it's also concerning that this reality isn't met by the obvious question: How did the eleven o'clock hour on Sunday mornings become segregated in the first place?

We need to *know the story* of race in America. We need to know the story of race and the church. We need to know one another's story. The stories we share matter. They tell us where we have been and offer an explanation on why we exist in the state we do.

History is often shortchanged and told from the lens of the majority, the powerful, or the perceived victors. It is revised, idealized, and anesthetized to fit the idea of goodness, projecting the story we want told about White America. We reduce it so much that we never dial into the horror that many experienced. The stories we tell shape who we are. That's why we need to learn the true stories.

Racism has shaped where we live, where we go to school, whom we interact with, and where we worship. We need to know how it all began and the economic implications of men owning men. We need to know the heartlessness of saying "Pull yourself up by your bootstraps" to a bootless man. We need to lean into one another and seek to understand with sincerity *how we got here.*

KNOW THE SIN TO NAME IT

When referring to racial justice, people often quote Amos 5:24: "Let justice roll on like a river, righteousness like a never-failing stream" (NIV). The passage makes clear what the Lord desires from Israel. But long before that justice, God, through Amos, focused on Israel's sin:

> For three transgressions of Israel,
>   and for four, I will not revoke the punishment,
> because they sell the righteous for silver,

and the needy for a pair of sandals—
those who trample the head of the poor into the dust of the
    earth
and turn aside the way of the afflicted;
a man and his father go in to the same girl,
    so that my holy name is profaned;
they lay themselves down beside every altar
    on garments taken in pledge,
and in the house of their God they drink
    the wine of those who have been fined. (Amos 2:6–8)

We, too, must name the sin. Each one of us have been short-changed on the topic of race in America. History and its impact have not been accurately portrayed to us. Thus, we exist in ignorance and continue to perpetuate harm toward one another.

Though a history of race in America, with an unvarnished portrayal of racial incidents, should be taught in school, a clear understanding of race, ethnicity, image bearing, and the complicity of the church in perpetuating this evil should be proclaimed in the church as well. We, too, own a part of this misgiving.

History is important to understand because it dictates so much of our present and future. Whether we recognize it or not, the past is present.

To move forward, we must begin by looking backward. We must explore history to fully understand the racial landscape of America and the West broadly. In doing so, we will more clearly locate ourselves in society and culture.

So let's take a look at some of the major events and ideas that have shaped us in significant ways.[4]

SLAVERY IN THE UNITED STATES

Where did race come from? How was it invented? While there isn't a specific moment in history we can point to as the beginning of this tragedy, we do know that Portugal initiated the transatlantic slave trade as early as in the fifteenth century, taking African people to work plantations in South America and the Caribbean, and other European countries followed suite after witnessing its economic benefits.[5] It was then that we began to see the budding and separation along skin colors. Nothing shaped and accelerated this caste system more than chattel slavery. African people, who bear the image of God, were reduced to being property, sold or forced aboard large ships to suffer their plight in cramped and inhumane conditions. Upon arriving to their destination, they were sold and subjected to physical abuse, rape, and harsh living conditions.

Slavery reached the shores of the British colonies in August 1619 at Jamestown, Virginia, with the arrival of more than twenty African people.[6] Those Africans were pirated from another vessel and forced aboard the *White Lion*, with an unsure destination. To get rid of the "cargo," the ship docked in North America and the Africans were sold and enslaved there, marking the beginning of the slave trade to what would become the United States.[7]

Slavery existed legally from 1619 to 1863 and was made illegal with the signing of the Emancipation Proclamation. However, it wasn't until June 19, 1865, that final enslaved people were freed within the United States jurisdiction. It would be a year later, June 14, 1866, that the final enslaved Africans were freed through treaties entered into by the United States regarding Indian territory.[8] That's 247 years of buying, selling, and trafficking people for financial gain.

By the conclusion of the slave trade, more than 12.5 million documented Africans were traded.[9] We are unsure how many undocumented African people were smuggled and traded. Additionally, about 15 percent, or nearly 2 million Africans died on the transatlantic voyage.[10]

Mothers, grandmothers, fathers, grandfathers, aunts, uncles, sisters, brothers, sons, daughters, and friends. It is easy for us to explore the data tied to slavery, and forget that this data is connected to individual image bearers who experienced unspeakable horrors. These stories must not be forgotten. They must be held closely, because ultimately we are part of the same fabric, made in the image of the Almighty. Consider Isabella and Anthony.

Isabella and Anthony were a part of the initial slaves brought to Jamestown in 1619 aboard the *White Lion*. They had been kidnapped from West Angola, stripped of their families, friends, and their native country, and forced aboard a ship headed for new lands. Once they arrived at Point Comfort (Jamestown), they were retained by the captain of the *White Lion*, William Tucker. Isabella and Anthony later married and started a family. While the details are unclear about the nature of their arrival and status after their arrival, one thing is sure, they were not free.[11]

The Economics of Slavery

The prosperity of the newly founded America was mostly dependent upon forced (free) labor. This labor not only supported individuals, but major institutions such as banks, universities, and various industries. For example, the largest bank in America, J. P. Morgan Chase, provided loans for mortgages and thousands of slaves, building the success of their business on slave capital.[12] The premiere academic institutions, such as Harvard and Yale, were funded with profits from slavery and related industries. And in some cases, such as with the University of Virginia, slaves literally built the buildings on campus and served faculty and students.[13]

And the insurance company Aetna sold policies to reimburse slave owners of their financial losses when slaves died.[14]

In 1850, slaves were worth about $1.3 billion, as each slave had a monetary value assigned based on their expected productivity, life expectancy, and skill set. By the time the Civil War began in 1861, there were approximately 4 million enslaved persons in the United States, worth just north of $4 billion. Enslaved people were considered more valuable than the nation's banks, factories, agricultural industry, and railroads combined.[15]

While much debate exists over the cause of the Civil War—from freeing enslaved people to fighting for states' right—one cause that is unquestionably true is that it was about economic *power* and maintaining that power. Free labor had a significant impact on one's bottom line.[16]

Exposing the Harsh Reality of Slavery

Frederick Douglass was born into slavery around 1818 and owned by Hugh Auld. Hugh is thought by many to be Frederick's father. Frederick himself suspected this possibility. Frederick's slave experience was unique in that from an early age, the plantation mistress, Sophia, taught him to read and write.

Hugh hated the idea that an enslaved person would learn. He knew the power of education—that one could not possibly remain enslaved if they began to understand the world around them. Not long after Hugh's objection, Sophia refused to teach Frederick further, hiding all reading materials and forbidding him to read. Frederick was then traded several times before he escaped to freedom around the age of twenty.[17]

In his autobiography, *Narrative of the Life of Frederick Douglass, an American Slave*, he recalls the moment in which his soul became liberated. In the middle of a beating, he stood up to his then master:

This battle with Mr. Covey was the turning-point in my career as a slave. It rekindled the few expiring embers of freedom, and revived within me a sense of my own manhood. It recalled the departed self-confidence, and inspired me again with a determination to be free. The gratification afforded by the triumph was a full compensation for whatever else might follow, even death itself. He only can understand the deep satisfaction which I experienced, who has himself repelled by force the bloody arm of slavery. I felt as I never felt before. It was a glorious resurrection, from the tomb of slavery, to the heaven of freedom. My long-crushed spirit rose, cowardice departed, bold defiance took its place; and I now resolved that, however long I might remain a slave in form, the day had passed forever when I could be a slave in fact. I did not hesitate to let it be known to me, that the white man who expected to succeed in whipping, must also succeed in killing me.[18]

Frederick spoke to the harsh realities of being broken as an enslaved person. He spoke to the degradation of the soul and will. He gives us insight into the pain of dehumanization that many enslaved persons could not give voice to. He describes, in almost spiritual terms, the freedom that was brought about through this experience.

Upon escaping enslavement, Frederick rose to fame and influence after giving a lecture at an abolitionist meeting that left the crowd mesmerized by his oratory skills. This was the beginning of Douglass's career, traveling abroad as a speaker and writer. His work served to enlighten people about the horror of slavery and the need for the liberation of Black people. It worked. Douglass is acclaimed as the most influential person and abolitionist of the nineteenth century.[19]

Frederick spoke of the dichotomy of being an enslaved person. The stripping of freedom, personhood, dignity, and humanity. Regarding the expectation that he should be thrilled about the second-class citizenry the enslaved had been relegated to, he writes:

> Yet, people in general, will say they like colored men as well as any other, but in their proper place! They assign us that place; they don't let us do it for ourselves, nor will they allow us a voice in the decision. They will not allow that we have a head to think, and a heart to feel, and a soul to aspire. They treat us not as men, but as dogs—they cry "Stu-boy!" and expect us to run and do their bidding. That's the way we are liked. You degrade us, and then ask why we are degraded— you shut our mouths, and then ask why we don't speak— you close our colleges and seminaries against us, and then ask why we don't know more.[20]

Later in life, Frederick penned a letter to his former master, Hugh Auld, rebuking him:

> How, let me ask, would you look upon me, were I, some dark night, in company with a band of hardened villains, to enter the precincts of your elegant dwelling, and seize the person of your own lovely daughter, Amanda, and carry her off from your family, friends, and all the loved ones of her youth—make her my slave—compel her to work, and I take her wages—place her name on my ledger as property— disregard her personal rights—fetter the powers of her immortal soul by denying her the right and privilege of learning to read and write—feed her coarsely—clothe her scantily, and whip her on the naked back occasionally;

more, and still more horrible, leave her unprotected—a
degraded victim to the brutal lust of fiendish overseers,
who would pollute, blight, and blast her fair soul—rob her
of all dignity—destroy her virtue, and annihilate in her
person all the graces that adorn the character of virtuous
womanhood? I ask, how would you regard me, if such were
my conduct?[21]

Frederick gives us a peek into the experience of an enslaved person. It draws a clear and painful illustration of what it must have been like to be enslaved. He reminds us that he and the millions of other enslaved people were in fact *human*. Humans who had been robbed of dignity, virtue, womanhood, manhood, and ultimately, personhood. This must be held with tremendous lament.

THE INDIAN REMOVAL ACT OF 1830

Each year on the second Monday in October, Americans celebrate the day that Christopher Columbus "discovered" America. There is but one problem with this notion: America was never lost in need of discovery. Columbus didn't discover anything. North American land was owned and occupied by Indigenous people for thousands of years. Starting with the arrival of Europeans, our Indigenous siblings have been robbed of land and freedom, had their possessions and businesses plundered, have been subjected to European practices, enslaved, watched helplessly as their women were raped, and experienced mass genocide in various ways. Theirs is a long, dark history of dehumanization and harm.

It is estimated that nearly 12 million native people existed at the time the colonies were settled. By the end of the nineteenth century, approximately 250,000 remained.[22] One of the most tragic events in our history with Indigenous people is the Indian Removal

Act of 1830, which led to the Trail of Tears and untold deaths. This act authorized President Andrew Jackson to remove Indigenous people from their desirable lands in the East and South and place them on prairie lands in the West beyond the Mississippi River. Many nations fell victim to this act's reach, including the Cherokee, Muscogee Creek, Chickasaw, Choctaw, Seminole, Wyandot, Kickapoo, Potawatomi, Shawnee, and Lenape tribes.[23] The reason for their removal was to capitalize on the fertile and desirable lands for agriculture and other industries. The White Southerners, including Jackson, wanted unrestricted access to the gold mines the Indigenous people possessed.[24]

Though the act guaranteed fair compensation to individuals to vacate the land, many were paid pennies on the dollar, manipulated, and swindled.[25]

The Indian Removal Act was also supposed to guarantee an orderly removal. After a period of attempting to deal with people who understandably didn't want to leave their land, President Jackson grew impatient and sent in reinforcements to forcibly remove residents and push them westward into territory inhabited by other Indians, and which would later be taken to found Oklahoma. The migrants faced hunger, disease, and exhaustion on their forced march along the Trail of Tears. Nearly fifteen thousand people died on the treacherous journey or at the hands of soldiers sent to escort and enforce the law.[26]

Making Light of Evil

My (Josh) wife, Lakisha, grew up in Broken Arrow, a suburb of Tulsa, Oklahoma. In grade school, her class learned about the Trail of Tears through an activity. She and her classmates were instructed to line up in a single-file line and to hold hands. The teacher presented each child with a Lunchable and had them store it in their backpacks. The students then traversed throughout the school and across a large field nearby, where they stopped on the journey and had lunch. After they ate, they resumed their travels, finally ending at the playground. The playground represented Oklahoma: the Indian territories "given" to the Indigenous people by the United States government. Did you catch that? The playground was their new frontier considered to be the land flowing with milk and honey—a gift. But this land was not a gift. It was a reminder that our Indigenous brothers and sisters' basic necessities and needs were secondary in priority to those who held all the power.

Taking a walk and eating a tasty Lunchable shapes the story into something palatable. But it neglects to share the truth of what happened and why. In a real sense, it then makes light of evil.

EMANCIPATION AND RECONSTRUCTION

On September 22, 1862, President Abraham Lincoln wrote an executive order, Proclamation 95, or as it is better known, the Emancipation Proclamation. It stipulates that on January 1, 1863, all enslaved people would be free:

> On the first day of January in the year of our Lord, one thousand eight hundred and sixty-three, all persons held as slaves within any State, or designated part of a State, the people whereof shall then be in rebellion against the United States shall be then, thenceforward, and forever free; and the executive government of the United States, including the military and naval authority thereof, will recognize and maintain the freedom of such persons, and will do no act or acts to repress such persons, or any of them, in any efforts they may make for their actual freedom.[27]

Though the order went into effect January 1, 1863, America was still in the middle of the Civil War. While some enslaved people were immediately emancipated, many more would not be liberated until the Union secured victory in the South. Even after the war, however, slavery was still practiced in various parts of the South until June 19, 1865, when the Union army rode into the final holdout in Galveston, Texas, and proclaimed victory and the liberation of the enslaved.

Today each year on June 19, African Americans continue to celebrate "Juneteenth," Freedom Day.

Afterward, for the next twelve years, opportunities to flourish appeared. The federal government passed amendments to the Constitution securing this freedom: the Thirteenth Amendment forbids slavery; the Fourteenth Amendment demands equal protection under the law; and the Fifteenth Amendment secures voting rights regardless of race or status.

Nearly two thousand African Americans held public office from the local level all the way up to the United States Senate.[28] Many African Americans could vote and participate in American democracy. Black universities, businesses, and communities emerged and flourished. It was a new day with their newfound freedom.

This period, however, wasn't all peace and prosperity. Though the Emancipation Proclamation and the war's end provided freedom, it didn't offer education on how to live free for many former enslaved people. Reconstruction, the period following the war, focused on rebuilding the war-torn country and working to heal the wounds, but in many cases African Americans were left to fend for themselves—they were freed all right, freed to experience famine. These individuals had no economic means and had known only life on the plantation, the life of an enslaved person. So upon emancipation, lacking economic means, many were subjugated by plantation owners, and essentially re-enslaved by being paid little to nothing.

And though the government put laws into place to secure freedom for African Americans, Southern governments wormed their way around those by enacting Black Codes, intended to maintain a White dominant social order and to ensure cheap labor for plantation owners.

Black Codes were akin to Slave Codes. Enslaved people were chattel, meaning they were property, they had no legal rights. Slave Codes were enacted to maintain order and instill fear into enslaved people to hedge against uprisings and escape attempts. Black Codes did much the same. Though varied from state to state, these codes in general treated African Americans as inferiors, relegating them to a subordinate position in society. Their right to own land was restricted, they could not bear arms, and they might be forced into servitude for vagrancy and other offenses. Violation or perceived violation of a Black Code carried severe punishment, including but not limited to fines, imprisonment by means of unpaid labor, and even death.

Worst of all, this period gave rise to racial terror and violence. The prosperity and freedom experienced by African Americans, coupled with the resentment of Confederate sympathizers and notions of white supremacy, gave rise to such organization as the Ku Klux Klan. The Klan's sole purpose was to intimidate Black people and restore White dominance in society. This period also gave rise to the public spectacles known as lynchings. During these years more than four thousand documented lynchings took place, with countless others that went undocumented.[29] There isn't a more gruesome and terrifying lynching story than that of Hayes, Mary, and Baby Turner.

Hayes, Mary, and Baby Turner

Hayes and Mary Turner were a young black couple living in the South around the turn of the twentieth century. Mary had two children she brought into their marriage. They worked together on a plantation in Brooks County, Georgia, owned by thirty-one-year-old Hampton Smith.

Hampton was notoriously mean, violent, abusive, and unfair toward his employees. Like many plantation owners, he leveraged the peonage system for free and cheap labor. Under Black Codes, he subjugated Black people, by paying their fines for petty crimes or offenses. In turn, he forced them to work on his plantation for little or no pay.

Nineteen-year-old Sydney Johnson was among the unfortunate recipients of Hampton's "charity." When Sydney was brought up on charges for gambling, Hampton paid his fines, bailing Sydney out of jail and forcing him into enslavement.[30]

When Sydney disputed his wages and then failed to work due to illness, Hampton beat him and refused to pay him the money owed for previous work he had completed. Not long after this incident, on May 18, 1918, Sydney allegedly shot and killed Hampton, though later this was disputed. The murder sparked a flurry of mob violence against people of color in search of Sydney and anyone else who may have been involved.

Because of Hayes's close association with Sydney, he was implicated as an accomplice. The mob apprehended and lynched him. As Mary, eight months pregnant, watched in shock at what they'd done to her innocent husband, she boldly proclaimed among the crowd that she would pursue legal action against the men who did this. Despite Mary's lack of legal standing as a Black person in the South, the mob said her remarks were "unwise" and pursued her.[31]

Mary fled for her life. The next day, however, she was caught and taken to Folsom Bridge, near Valdosta, Georgia. There the mob hung her upside down by her ankles, doused her with gasoline, and set her on fire to burn off her clothing. Then one of those involved took a butcher's knife and cut Mary's unborn child from her womb, spilling the baby on the payment. The eight-month-old child let out several cries before one of the men crushed the baby with his boot. Mary, who was still alive, was then shot more than one hundred times by the mob.[32]

Sydney, Hayes, Mary, Baby Turner, and the nine other people killed in this lynching rampage matter. Their stories bear witness to the evil of racism.

There are countless stories like the Turners' story. Stories of tremendous pain, devastation, and terror. Stories that you and I have never heard. Growing up in Tulsa in the nineties, I (Josh) heard almost nothing about lynchings and Jim Crow in school. And what I did hear on slavery was shared through a reductionist lens. We were duped into believing it wasn't really that bad. And if we believe that misinformation, we may not feel any residual impact and no need for us to act.

Ida B. Wells

One woman who understood the evil of racism and acted on it was Ida B. Wells. Ida Belle Wells was born into slavery in 1862 in Holly Springs, Mississippi, and was freed by the Emancipation Proclamation. Wells came of age during Reconstruction and lived through the peak of the backlash of White supremacy.

At sixteen years of age, Ida lost both of her parents to yellow fever and assumed responsibility for her five siblings. To be near extended family, she moved her and her siblings to Memphis, Tennessee. Here she witnessed the continued inhumane treatment of freed Blacks, causing her to become a fierce advocate of civil rights.

In 1884, after being forcibly removed from a rail car for refusing to leave the "ladies' car" to move to the smoking car, where Blacks were expected to sit, Ida filed a lawsuit challenging the legality of segregation of railroad cars. Initially, she won the case. However, the Supreme Court of Tennessee overturned it. But her experience lit a fire within her.

Five years later, in 1889, Ida became co-partner of the *Free Speech and Headlight* newspaper along with Rev. R. Nightingale, pastor of Beale Street Baptist Church. With this new platform, she began to write about the disenfranchisement and violence against Black people.[33]

After the lynching of her friend Thomas Moss and two others in 1891, Ida began speaking out about lynching. Speaking at the National Negro Conference in June 1909, she said, "No other nation, civilized or savage, burns its criminals; only under that Stars and Stripes is the human holocaust possible. Twenty-eight human beings burned at the stake, one of them a woman and two of them children, is the awful indictment against American civilization— the gruesome tribute which the nation pays to the color line."[34]

Frederick Douglass said of her, "Thank you for your faithful paper on the lynch abomination now generally practiced against colored people in the South. There has been no word equal to it in convincing power. I have spoken, but my word is feeble in comparison."[35]

For the rest of her life she would prove to be an effective racial and gender justice activist, investigative journalist, and women's rights proponent. She was also one of the founding members of the National Association for the Advancement of Colored People (NAACP) and the National Association of Women of Color.[36]

JIM CROW: SEPARATE, BUT EQUAL

Reconstruction and Black Codes were followed by Jim Crow "laws," beginning in 1877. Jim Crow is named after a minstrel routine "Jump Jim Crow." The routine was performed in black face and later became a derogatory epithet for Black people. Jim Crow was cemented in the landmark case Plessy v. Ferguson in 1896. The Supreme Court's decision codified the idea of "separate, but equal," relegating the effects of the Fourteenth Amendment useless in protecting the equal rights of Black Americans.

Jim Crow relegated Black people to permanent inferior status. Though it was called separate but equal, it always meant separate and inferior. Jim Crow laws required separate accommodations for Black people, and for people of color broadly. Public parks, theaters, restaurants, buses, train stations, train cars, water fountains, restrooms, pools, phone booths, hospitals, asylums, jails, building entrances, even cemeteries were all segregated. It was common place to see signs posted at town and city limits warning African Americans that they were not welcome there.

The Jim Crow period extended in the 1950s and 1960s. The dismantling of this evil began with the victory in the Brown v. Board of Education Topeka case in 1954. It was dealt its final blow in 1964 with the passage of The Civil Rights Act, in 1965 with the Voting Rights Act, and with the Fair Housing Act of 1968. Just a little more than fifty years ago—recent history.

Yet even in the midst of Jim Crow, its effects gave rise to the most notable civil rights leaders such as W. E. B. Du Bois, Thurgood Marshall, Coretta Scott King, James Meredith, Rosa Parks, and Dr. Martin Luther King, Jr., as well as many more heroes and heroines who largely go unmentioned—the brave men and women who sat at lunch counters, integrated schools, and withstood vicious assaults on their humanity. Ella Baker is one such heroine.

Ella Baker

Born in 1903, Ella Baker was inspired by the resilience of her grandparents who spent most of their lives enslaved. She led a life filled with advocacy on behalf of Black people and Black women in particular. She first served as the national director of the Young Negros Cooperative League. Next, she went on to become the highest-ranking woman of the NAACP. There she spent much of her time organizing national chapters, raising money, and pursuing grassroots voting efforts. Known as personable and charismatic, grateful and grit-full, it is here that Ella created a name for herself.

She was also involved in forming the Southern Christian Leadership Council (SCLC), led by Dr. King. She served as the associate director and the interim executive director for two years. Under her leadership, the SCLC made a significant impact, growing and organizing local and national efforts. But she found her time there frustrating. The organization was steeped in patriarchy and relied heavily on one central charismatic figure, Dr. King. Still she was committed to the work and left an indelible mark through her efforts organizing nonviolent protests, voter registrations, and fundraising on behalf of the organization.

In 1960, after hearing about the sit-ins led by college students, Ella initiated a relationship between SCLC and what would become the Student Nonviolent Coordinating Committee (SNCC). She was instrumental in founding the organization, providing leadership, and giving substance to the movement. During her time there, she paved the way for leaders such as Marrion Barry, Julian Bond, John Lewis, Stokely Carmichael, Diane Nash, and Bob Moses. It is through her influence that SNCC became one of the foremost civil rights and human rights organizations in the world. She is also credited as the backbone of organizing and mobilizing efforts to see the Civil Rights Act of 1965 come to pass.[37]

Later, along with Fannie Lou Hamer and Bob Moses, she went on to co-found the Mississippi Freedom Democratic Party. Though largely unrecognized for her contributions, Ella made a tremendous impact on the freedoms that people of color have come to enjoy.[38]

Ella would say of herself: "You didn't see me on television, you didn't see news stories about me. The kind of role that I tried to play was to pick up pieces or put together pieces out of which I hoped organization might come. My theory is, strong people don't need strong leaders."[39]

THE STRUGGLE CONTINUES

The civil rights period of the fifties and sixties put an end to overt legislated, systemic racism. Where slavery, Black Codes, Jim Crow, and restrictive laws relegated Black people, people of color broadly, and women to second-class citizenship, this period brought about a new day. Many of the liberties we experience today are possible only because of bravery and persistence of countless men and women, to whom we owe a debt of gratitude.

The post-civil rights period has also brought with it great challenges. In a world where equality is possible, many have taken a colorblind approach, as if the Civil Rights and Voting Rights Acts alleviated residual effects of legislated racism. Further, it has even led some to believe that racism is no more. As evinced by history, we must expect, measure, and address the evolution of racism to ensure that progress continues.

While we may be able to share space together, attend the same schools, and vote for elected officials, racism never went away, it merely morphed and became more sophisticated.

Let's consider for a moment the history of America in mathematical terms. From the founding of the first permanent American

> We have many years of pursuing equality and repair before we can expect to be on solid ground.

settlement in 1607 through 2021 is 414 years. Slavery lasted 246 years. Black Codes and Jim Crow lasted 103 years, until 1968 with the passage of the Fair Housing Act. That's a total of 349 years, or 86 percent, of US history steeped in legislated racism dating back to the colonial period. More than three centuries of history characterized by violence, dehumanization, and tyranny.

Let's suppose that I (Josh) were married ten years, and 86 percent of my marriage was steeped in hate, violence, exploitation, and hurt. Should I expect the next 14 percent, or 1.5 years, where equality was possible—not pursued, but possible—to be free of conflict and residual trauma? Will the 14 percent undo the trauma of our history together?

It is the same with the American Experiment. Eighty-six percent of our marriage is steeped in horrific events. For 86 percent of our marriage, people of color were prostitutes and exploited. Murdered and maimed. Assaulted and dehumanized. We have many years of pursuing equality and repair before we can expect to be on solid ground. If it took at least 349 years for us to create this mess, we must calibrate our expectation that it could take years of intentionality before life, liberty, and the pursuit of happiness is possible and experienced by all people. This history proves that racism is more a part of who we are than we like to give credit for. May God hasten the day when we outlive the evils of the past and embrace our future as one people, united by God, indivisible, that justice may reign for all.

4

Know the Story of the Church

Everyone talks about Dr. King's paramount work, *Letter from a Birmingham Jail*. Almost no one talks about the letter that provoked Dr. King's response. Here it is:

> We clergymen are among those who, in January, issued "An Appeal for Law and Order and Common Sense," in dealing with racial problems in Alabama. We expressed understanding that honest convictions in racial matters could properly be pursued in the courts, but urged that decisions of those courts should in the meantime be peacefully obeyed.
>
> Since that time there has been some evidence of increased forbearance and a willingness to face facts. Responsible citizens have undertaken to work on various problems which caused racial friction and unrest. In Birmingham, recent public events have given indication that

we all have opportunity for a new constructive and realistic approach to racial problems.

However, we are now confronted by a series of demonstrations by some of our Negro citizens, directed and led in part by outsiders. We recognize the natural impatience of people who feel that their hopes are slow in being realized. But we are convinced that these demonstrations are unwise and untimely.

We agree rather with certain local Negro leadership which has called for honest and open negotiation of racial issues in our area. And we believe this kind of facing of issues can best be accomplished by citizens of our own metropolitan area, white and Negro, meeting with their knowledge and experiences of the local situation. All of us need to face that responsibility and find proper channels for its accomplishment.

Just as we formerly pointed out that "hatred and violence have no sanction in our religious and political tradition," we also point out that such actions as incite to hatred and violence, however technically peaceful those actions may be, have not contributed to the resolution of our local problems. We do not believe that these days of new hope are days when extreme measures are justified in Birmingham.

We commend the community as a whole, and the local news media and law enforcement officials in particular, on the calm manner in which these demonstrations have been handled. We urge the public to continue to show restraint should the demonstrations continue, and the law enforcement officials to remain calm and continue to protect our city from violence.

We further strongly urge our own Negro community to

withdraw support from these demonstrations, and to unite locally in working peacefully for a better Birmingham. When rights are consistently denied, a cause should be pressed in the courts and in negotiations among local leaders, and not in the streets. We appeal to both our white and Negro citizenry to observe the principles of law and order and common sense.[1]

This letter was penned in April 1963, by a cohort of all White, Christian (and one Jewish) men. This same year brought the assassination of civil rights activist Medgar Evers (June 12); and the 16th Street Baptist Church bombing (September 15), which claimed the lives of four little girls: fourteen-year-olds Addie Mae Collins, Carole Rosamond Robertson, Cynthia Dionne Wesley, and eleven-year-old Carol Denise McNair.[2]

It was the same year that in his inauguration speech, the governor of Alabama, George Wallace, declared, "Segregation now, segregation tomorrow, segregation forever."[3] This was the same governor who later that year physically obstructed the entrance of the University of Alabama, refusing Black students Vivian Malone and James Hood from attending.[4]

In this same year peaceful protestors, including women and children, were attacked by police, brutalized by police dogs, and blasted by high-powered water hoses. And Dr. King was arrested for leading a peaceful protest. It was also in 1963 that he penned some of his most poignant and prophetic words in response to this group of clergy in his "Letter from a Birmingham Jail," as well as his iconic "I Have a Dream" speech.

This was the height of the fight for civil rights, and it was Birmingham that represented the worst of Southern racism and Jim Crow. And members of the church were standing on the wrong side of the battle, as we see in this letter from the clergy.

Certainly these clergy thought they were doing good. But good intentions often miscarry into bad outcomes when not calibrated with respect to people's lived realities, love, or sound theological understanding. We can have the best intentions, but like these clergy, history will portray us to be lovers of comfort, rejectors of holy disruption, and tone-deaf to the clear invitation that the gospel makes to love one another, affirming the imago Dei impressed upon every man and woman, girl and boy.

Dr. King's response reflected such a sentiment:

> I must make two honest confessions to you, my Christian and Jewish brothers. First, I must confess that over the past few years I have been gravely disappointed with the white moderate. I have almost reached the regrettable conclusion that the Negro's great stumbling block in his stride toward freedom is not the White Citizen's Counciler or the Ku Klux Klanner, but the white moderate, who is more devoted to "order" than to justice; who prefers a negative peace which is the absence of tension to a positive peace which is the presence of justice; who constantly says: "I agree with you in the goal you seek, but I cannot agree with your methods of direct action"; who paternalistically believes he can set the timetable for another man's freedom; who lives by a mythical concept of time and who constantly advises the Negro to wait for a "more convenient season." Shallow understanding from people of good will is more frustrating than absolute misunderstanding from people of ill will. Lukewarm acceptance is much more bewildering than outright rejection.[5]

As opposed to condemning the heinous and egregious acts of de jure and de facto segregation and racism, these ministers and rabbi took a passive apathetic approach. Essentially they said, "Be patient and have a good attitude while you suffer injustice. Don't rock the boat. Trust the very system that relegates you to second-class citizenship to be the one who will make things right for you." This response typified the White moderate in those days and in the present. White moderate, meaning those Whites who are slow or unwilling to stand to defend or speak up in times of injustice; those who prefer not to mess with the status quo. They are not outright racist. In fact, they may adamantly *agree* that racism is wrong. Yet they cleave to their comfort and shun any racial disruption. They are content to be "not racist" yet unwilling to support the full liberation and dignification of people of color.

> While some claim the church lost its way, lost its prophetic voice and conscience when it comes to matters of racial injustice, we contend that the majority of the church has been lost all along.

As Dr. King stated, White moderates, in many ways, are worse than blatant racists—because their silence in the fight undermines the work of justice and ultimate peace and reconciliation.

It's bad enough to have White moderates in society; it's inexcusable to have them in the church.

RACISM AND ITS ACCOMPLICE, THE CHURCH

While some claim the church lost its way, lost its prophetic voice and conscience when it comes to matters of racial injustice, we contend that the majority of the church has been lost all along. It did not look at the Scriptures to see the role of the good Samaritan and follow the *mercy* of God toward humankind. It did not take seriously the promise to Abraham that God would give a *multitude* of people as his inheritance (see Rom. 4:16). It didn't take seriously the aberration of injustice and corruption concerning the nation of Israel in the book of Amos. It never came to see with clarity that the King of the universe has always been concerned about righteousness and justice, so much so that He founded His throne upon these truths.

Because of their inaction and failure to follow Christ, the church has been an accomplice to racism. We did not behold the reality of our eschatological future, that we human beings are ethnically and culturally diverse, and this is not a mistake or the result of the fall but by God's marvelous design. Yes, by and large, we have been lost all along.

And the world noticed. Here's how Frederick Douglass reflected upon the church:

> I therefore hate the corrupt, slaveholding, women-whipping, cradle-plundering, partial and hypocritical Christianity of the land.... I look upon it as the climax of all misnomers, the boldest of all frauds, and the grossest of all libels. Never was there a clearer case of "stealing the livery of the court of heaven to serve the devil in." I am filled with unutterable loathing when I contemplate the religious pomp and show, together with the horrible inconsistencies, which everywhere surround me. We have men-stealers for ministers, women-whippers for missionaries, and cradle-plunderers for church members.... The dealer gives his blood-stained gold to support the pulpit, and the pulpit, in return, covers his infernal business with the garb of Christianity. Here we have religion and robbery the allies of each other—devils dressed in angels' robes, and hell presenting the semblance of paradise.[6]

Douglass's notice of "the horrible inconsistencies" within the church represent what many observe. What a tragedy to we who have been called to be the light and salt.

But the story doesn't have to end there. In fact, it doesn't end there. Many faithful believers have stood up and spoken prophetically. It is because of their audacity to believe that we can and should be a better witness that we have made progress to the present moment. Are things perfect? No. We have many miles to travel and much work to do, but we can emerge as the beautiful bride adorned in glory and splendor. That means first we must *know* the story of our American church history as if relates to racial matters—reflecting over some of the ways we have gotten it wrong—and right—so we can learn, reconcile, and move into the future in strength.

Let's look at a few of those "horrible inconsistencies" the church has been guilty of.

JUSTIFYING SLAVERY: THE CURSE OF HAM

Noah, his family, and all the animals had exited the ark. After forty days aboard and the extinction of the rest of humanity, Noah thought, *I need a glass of wine*. So he planted a vineyard, and made the drink from its harvest. Noah drank to excess, and in his drunken stupor, he passed out and lay naked, which his son Ham, "the father of Canaan," saw (see Gen. 9:22–25). When Noah awoke and learned what his youngest son had done, he said, "Cursed be Canaan! The lowest of slaves will he be to his brothers" (v. 25 NIV).

Noah was disappointed with his son's actions and cursed Ham's offspring, Canaan. To be clear, Ham was never cursed, Ham's son Canaan was. And if you recall the notorious Canaanites from Scripture, you know they were among Israel's biggest foes, who ultimately suffered defeat and ceased to exist as a nation.

Yet many American Christians during the time of slavery took this story and manipulated it to focus on *Ham* being cursed. More so, they identified his name as meaning "darker one," as in he was darker than his siblings—though theological scholarship doesn't support this claim. Many within the church argued that Ham's darker skin must mean God cursed Black people of African descent, because they are dark. This became the "Curse of Ham"—giving life and credence to slavery, justifying it, and further entrenching it.[7]

Consider this thought from Patrick Mell, president of the Southern Baptist Convention (1863–1871 and 1880–1887): "From Ham were descended the nations that occupied the land of Canaan and those that now constitute the African or Negro race. Their inheritance, according to prophecy, has been and will continue to be slavery. . . . [And] so long as we have the Bible . . . we expect to maintain it."[8]

This was our witness to the world. Christians took holy Scripture and manipulated it to justify the oppression and dehumanization of people—people for whom Christ died and gave full rights to be heirs in His kingdom.

KEY WHITE MODERATE CHRISTIANS AND THEIR IMPACT ON THE RACIAL LANDSCAPE

Of course our intention is not to lump all American Christians into one category and suggest that everyone was a racist or a moderate. History shows us, however, that many Christians did struggle with the issue. For instance, sociologist and scholar Michael Emerson pointed out, "On the whole, northern evangelicals did not differ from southern evangelicals in their racial views, except that they tended to oppose slavery."[9]

As we look at a few examples of notable leaders of the faith, we see that even they not only struggled with being moderate, but in some instances, actually committed dreadful sins against Black brothers and sisters. And those decisions affected the racial landscape of the country and of the church, harming their brothers and sisters of color.

George Whitefield

The late eighteenth century was a period in which Christianity, in the words of Michael Emerson, "had grown stale."[10] The country was ready for spiritual revival. And it came through the first Great Awakening, of which George Whitefield played a significant part.

Whitefield, hailed as America's first celebrity preacher, is thought to be the hero founder of evangelicalism and greatly shaped the culture of Christianity.[11] He also spoke plainly about slavery and Black people. According to Jemar Tisby, Whitefield "excoriated enslavers for their physical abuse of slaves, calling them 'monsters of barbarity.'"[12] Additionally, he presented the gospel to Black people when his contemporaries argued that they didn't even have souls. He defended his position, explaining that Black people by nature are the same as their White counterparts: "Are your children, anyway better by nature than the poor negroes? No, in no wise. Blacks are just as much, and no more, conceived and born in sin, as white men are. Both if born and bred up here, I am persuaded, are naturally capable of the same religious improvement."[13]

But his stance eventually changed to "benefit" the work he was doing when he started the Bethesda Orphanage in his home colony of Georgia. Though the colony was founded as an antislavery territory, Whitefield believed and stated firmly that "Georgia can never be a flourishing province unless negroes are employed as slaves."[14] Whitefield saw Georgia's antislavery position as a snare in his path toward the success of the orphanage, since he wanted slave labor to keep the orphanage up and running rather than relying on paid help. So strong were his sentiments that he took action, testifying before England's Parliament in support of introducing slavery in Georgia.[15]

He argued that God had created the hot Georgia climate for Black people, that Great Britain's sizeable investment there would be lost without increased production, "that the orphanage would not survive without the benefit of slaves, and, consistent with his call, the unsaved would become saved."[16] He justified his new stance, believing that bringing Black people to the colonies as slaves would benefit God's kingdom, that God in His great wisdom ordained for Black people to be exported from Africa to be proselytized into the Christian faith.

Charles Finney

The nineteenth century saw a second Great Awakening and a hero in the fight for the dignity of Black and Brown people— Charles Finney. Finney was a riveting preacher and a trailblazer. He is considered the father of the modern revival movement, paving the way for the likes of D. L. Moody and Billy Graham. A lawyer turned evangelist, his impact was significant, as everywhere he preached, religious zeal took hold and a great number of conversions occurred. He was also staunch in his stance against slavery, contributing substantially to the abolitionist movement. According to Michael Emerson:

> He supplied the theological framework—stressing the need for the devout to engage social reform—and the revivalistic impulse for opposition to slavery. That is, he made opposition to slavery an aspect of Christian discipleship. Many of

the prominent abolitionists were influenced by him. Finney not only preached the evil of slaveholding, but was one of the first to use his pulpit to prohibit slaveholders from taking communion, claiming that those who owned slaves were not Christians.[17]

Willing to stand strong for what he deemed the right thing to do, he went further than many of his contemporaries. And yet, though he leveraged his pulpit to speak against the institution of slavery, he maintained segregation in the church, even disallowing Black people to vote on church matters or participate in communion.

Billy Graham

Billy Graham was known as America's pastor. He gave leadership to the broader part of the Evangelical movement. He provided counsel to twelve sitting presidents in his more than eighty years of ministry. He boldly proclaimed the gospel of Jesus Christ to filled arenas throughout the entire world. And in the midst of Jim Crow, he unabashedly removed the ropes of segregation from his Chattanooga, Tennessee, crusade in 1953, calling for integration at his gatherings a year ahead of the landmark integration legislation, *Brown v. Topeka Board of Education*, in 1954. Since Graham felt that God's eternal kingdom wouldn't be segregated, neither should his crusade meetings. He demanded that the ropes of segregation come down, and when the head usher refused, Graham removed the ropes himself.[18] From that moment forward for the rest of his ministry, Graham maintained integrated crusades. Additionally, he consistently preached on the need for love across racial lines and the gospel being the solution for racism.

And yet he struggled with actively pursuing an end to racism outside the bounds of personal salvation. Dr. King said of Graham:

You have courageously brought the Christian gospel to bear on the question of race in all of its urgent dimensions. You, above any other preacher in America, can open the eyes of many persons on this question. Your tremendous popularity, your extensive influence and your powerful message give you an opportunity in the area of human rights above almost any other person that we can point to. Your message in this area has additional weight because you are a native southerner.[19]

King was encouraging Graham to speak up and lead the way. And in 1957 Graham invited King to share at his crusade in New York City. Things seemed fine until a year later when news broke that Price Daniel, the segregationist governor of Texas, was set to introduce Graham at a crusade in San Antonio. King wrote to Graham, "Under the circumstances we would hope that Governor Daniel's participation in your program might be avoided. If this is not done, we urge you to make crystal clear your position on this burning moral issue."[20]

In response, Grady Wilson, one of Graham's aides and close friends replied:

We were surprised to receive your telegram and learn of your feelings toward the Governor of the Sovereign State of Texas. Even though we do not see eye to eye with him on every issue, we still love him in Christ, and frankly, I think that should be your position not only as a Christian but as a minister of the Gospel of our risen Lord.

Perhaps you should know that we received scores of letters and telegrams concerning your coming to our meeting in New York, and yet Mr. Graham was happy to have you come as a fellow minister in Christ.[21]

In 1961 after King participated in his first sit-in—a peaceful demonstration meant to raise awareness around segregation—and was subsequently arrested for it, a reporter asked Graham about the civil rights movement and MLK. Graham remarked, "I do believe that we have a responsibility to obey the law. Otherwise, you have anarchy. And no matter what that law may be—it may be an unjust law—I believe we have a Christian responsibility to obey it."[22]

Later in 1963, he commented to the *New York Times* on the Birmingham marches and protests, as well as King's imprisonment. He urged his "good and personal friend" to "put the brakes on a little bit." And he had "serious doubt . . . that the Negro community there supports it."[23]

And in response to Dr. King's iconic "I Have a Dream" speech—in which King said, "I have a dream that one day, down in Alabama little black boys and black girls will be able to join hands with little white boys and white girls as sisters and brothers"—Graham stated, "Only when Christ comes again will the little white children of Alabama walk hand in hand with little black children."[24]

Whether Graham intended it or not, his absence from the civil rights movement and his silence concerning the perils facing Black and Brown men and women spoke volumes. Graham desired gradualism and nonconfrontational action. His sentiment was much the same nearly thirty years after King's assassination. In 1996 Graham stated, "[King] had his demonstrations in the street, while I had mine as lawful religious services in stadiums."[25]

It's worth wondering how much further in the journey toward a reconciled nation and church would we be if these two prolific figures had worked together. Consider the possibilities if Graham would have sold out to the cause, advocating for the full liberation and dignification of Black people in America.

The indifference of the White moderate has a cost. In the case of Graham, he preached freedom from individual sin but did nothing to help free them from the sin of discrimination and legislated racist sin being perpetrated against them.

HOLY DISRUPTORS

In the midst of the church's overall tolerance of racist behaviors and attitudes, there were many holy disruptors who spoke out in prophetic ways and engaged the battle for justice. Many are unsung heroes known but to God. Others made the history books, such as Dr. King. We need to know these stories too because they help motivate, encourage, and navigate us to reach for continued progress.

Richard Allen

Throughout our years in ministry—both directly in the church and in Christian organizations—we've heard on many occasions, "Isn't it racist for the Black church to exist? I mean, if we are going to talk to the White church, we ought to speak to the racist existence of this institution as well."

Each time, I (Josh) reply, "I would say that the Black church testifies to God's kindness and providence, in that He would not allow a damnable system of dehumanization to prevent the advancement of the gospel among Black people and that He used the Black church to pave a path toward justice and the liberation of Black and Brown people. In fact, the Black church stands as a rebuke to the broader Evangelical movement."

Richard Allen is one such holy disruptor God used in mighty ways to help found the Black church.

Allen was a pioneer and the patriarch of the Black church in the West. Born in Philadelphia in 1760, he came to know Christ at the age of seventeen and began preaching shortly thereafter. Allen even proclaimed the gospel to his "owner," who soon came into a saving knowledge of Jesus Christ. Allen's owner was so impressed with him that he allowed Allen to purchase his freedom. Thereafter, Allen began preaching wherever he was welcomed, mainly within the Methodist preaching circuit. Notable leaders like Francis Asbury paved the way for Allen, ensuring he had a place to preach.

In 1786, Allen joined St. George's Methodist Church in Philadelphia. His Black presence and charisma caused an influx of Black people to flock to the services.[26] Until the late eighteenth century, many churches were welcoming to Black people and did not require segregation in seating or worship. Although Black parishioners did not have voting power, couldn't be ordained as elders, or administer the sacraments, they were allowed to be integrated in worship. Such was the case at St. George's, until one Sunday in 1787 when some church trustees grew concerned over the rise of Black attendees. Without notice, they decided to segregate Black believers into an upstairs gallery. While the Black believers were kneeling in prayer, one of the trustees grabbed Absolam Jones, a friend of Allen's and fellow pioneer of the Black church, insisting that he and the others move. The man's actions resulted in Jones and Allen, along with the Black parishioners, to leave the church.[27]

Shortly after this exit Jones and Allen, along with several others, formed the Free African Society (FAS). FAS sought to support escaped slaves seeking freedom. Allen and Jones continued pioneering this work, which gave rise to the first Black-led Episcopal church in the nation on July 17, 1794. A little more than twenty years later, Jones and Allen went on to found the first African American denomination, the African Methodist Episcopal

Church. Their courageous exit from St. George's Cathedral on that Sunday led to an exodus that gave rise to the formalization of Black church in America.

The Black church emerged as a safe haven for Black Christians, one that respected the full dignification of all Black people in America. The Black church also emerged as the prophetic body that led the way toward freedom from slavery, liberation from Jim Crow, and worked to correct policies that harmed Black and Brown communities.

Soon integrated worship ended as more and more churches began to segregate Whites and Blacks, especially after the Civil War. A byproduct of this choice was that relations between White and Black Christians grew harsher and more distant. That, in turn, led to Black and White people congregating separately—a condition that continues in many places throughout the United States to this day. But as Jemar Tisby notes: "While black Christians left white churches and denominations en masse after the Civil War, the formation of African Methodist Episcopal Church (AME) stands as an early example of Black Christians exercising agency to escape racism in the church and form their own more affirming fellowships."[28] Black people needed a safe haven, and the Black church became the space for them to experience dignity and worship without restriction.[29]

The Black church has stood in stark contrast to a large part of the church in the West. It testifies of God's faithfulness to Black people in that He would raise up a voice, which would pave the way for more voices to be heard, which would lead to the civil rights movement, a gospel movement, making it possible for the moment we live in today. Thank God for Richard Allen, Absolam Jones, and the Black church, for they remind us of God's providence, grace, and love for all of His people.

Harriet Beecher Stowe

Harriet Beecher Stowe was the daughter and sister of two notable preachers and abolitionists, her father Rev. Lyman Beecher and her brother Henry Ward Beecher. She was a devout Christian woman and spent her entire life as an activist, following in the footsteps of her father. She saw slavery as abhorrent and believed that abolishing it was the only path forward.

One night she had a dream that depicted the brutality of slavery. Writer and historian David S. Reynold writes that she "saw four figures: an old slave being whipped to death by two fellow slaves, who were goaded on by a brutal white man."[30]

The enslaved man being brutalized would become Tom, the central character in her book, *Uncle Tom's Cabin*. Initially published in an anti-slavery newspaper in forty-one installments, later it was compiled into a two-volume book that became the bestselling book of the nineteenth century, second only to the Bible.[31]

While there are parts of this work that some rightly take issue with, we must acknowledge how progressive this work was for the period and how instrumental it was in bringing about the Civil War, which ultimately ended slavery. It has been said that President Abraham Lincoln teased Stowe with starting the Civil War. Upon meeting her, he said, "So you're the little woman that started this great war!"[32]

Her work gave White Americans a push in the right direction. She presented an opportunity for them to see the horrors of slavery, affirming their suspicions, and swaying the opinion of the masses.

You

God is calling you to be a holy disruptor. The Western church has found itself at another inflection point, and if we get it right, history will speak well of us. If we get it mostly right yet never stand clearly for reconciliation, justice, and righteousness, there will always be an asterisk next to our moment in history in which we allowed our calling to pass us by.

> Reconcilers don't only stand against an evil, they stand for something bigger and greater than themselves.

It simply isn't enough to identify as not racist, wanting to put as much distance as you can between you and the idea of racism. That, our friend, is acting as a moderate. And we've seen in this chapter, the damage moderates can do to the work of God's kingdom.

So here is the question: Where do you stand? Are you merely against racism, or are you for reconciliation? Are you merely against bigotry, or are you for bridge building? Are you merely against prejudice, or are you for peacemaking?

Reconcilers don't only stand against an evil, they stand for something bigger and greater than themselves. And in the act of standing, they disrupt the status quo and change the landscape for good. They stand for the full dignification of all people. They fight and raise their voices in the spirit of Dr. Martin Luther King, Jr., Harriet Beecher Stowe, Richard Allen, and countless others.

Though the church hasn't always gotten it right, we have hope in her. History has proven that a faithful few willing to be forerunners *can* produce change, revival, and reform. You can be that person too. You can be a holy disruptor and change the landscape for good.

5

Know One Another's Stories

The first time OneRace assembled local pastors for prayer across racial and denominational lines, few in the room knew one another. Rather than jumping into prayer, we took time to talk and get to know one another. Leaders, often accustomed to going it alone, opened their hearts concerning ministry and family challenges. As our time together continued, we realized that though we'd gathered to pray for God to move in our city, we could not do that without first knowing one another as brothers and sisters.

We have seen how we must know the history of race in our nation and how the church reacted to that issue. Now we turn our attention to knowing our own place in that story and in the stories of those around us. As George Santayana said in a speech to the House of Commons, "Those who fail to learn from history are doomed to repeat it." Knowing the errors of the past provide the opportunity to *learn from them* and apply what we have learned in real life. We must examine our own generation's part of the story that is still being told, individually and collectively. We cannot do this in isolation. It requires self-reflection, trust, proximity, and intentionality within community as essential elements of living reconciled.

We cannot be reconcilers without building truly reconciled relationships. One of the deceptions of education is that it can make you feel as though you are doing something without actually ever doing anything. Of course it is easier to feel as though we "love our neighbor" when we haven't really had to deal with them. Another temptation is to attend church with people of other races, pray for reconciliation, and be among people of other races, and think of yourself as living reconciled. But that doesn't produce true reconciliation. To live reconciled we must go beyond surface-level interactions to form truly vulnerable heart-level relationships.

> One of the deceptions of education is that it can make you feel as though you are doing something without actually ever doing anything.

Building real relationships is messy work. We must not settle for a form of reconciliation that assuages the conscience with the appearance of unity but avoids the hard work of building enduring relationships.

To experience life- and culture-changing reconciled relationships, we need to embrace four vital ingredients that will help us navigate *knowing* better, and will in turn strengthen us as we move forward into *owning* and *changing*. At the heart of each of these ingredients is resiliency. Why is that essential? Because invariably we will experience conflict—within ourselves and with others. There are few people I (Hazen) have had more conflict with than my dear friend Josh, because we have spent lots of time together, because our reconciliation work is hard, and because we have a friendship we know can endure healthy conflict. That's resiliency.

Now let's look at the four ingredients we need.

INGREDIENT #1: SELF-REFLECTION

A few years ago, I (Hazen) attended a leadership conference for church planters hosted at an African American church in Atlanta, where the vast majority of attendees were African American. The worship was different and I was unfamiliar with many of the songs, the leaders and speakers often made cultural references everyone else got but I didn't understand, and I experienced a style of communication that at times was very different from what I was used to. While I loved the conference and learned so much from the presenters, I also realized I had never been in a training environment where I was the overwhelming *minority*. For that weekend I felt the pressure that so many of my friends of minority culture feel as they work to adapt and fit in. After the conference, I knew I needed to do some self-reflection to consider how being in that different cultural environment made me feel and why.

As we seek to live reconciled lives, we must start with knowing and accepting our own journeys. We all have a racial identity, but for those who are in the majority, we can often feel that we *don't* have a unique racial culture because we are not faced with a contrasting experience in our daily lives. What others experience as "White culture" is the norm for us, and that makes it difficult to distinguish its unique characteristics, both positive and negative. Trying to explain to many White people that they have a unique culture would be like trying to explain to a fish that it can breathe underwater. Only when the fish comes out of the water does it realize what that truly means.

There is a great exercise OneRace often presents at workshops. We first learned of it from our friend Bethaney Wilkinson, leader of the Diversity Gap Academy. The first time I went through this exercise, Bethaney distributed sticky notes and asked us to write what we'd learned about Black people from our parents and grandparents, and then what we'd learned about White people from our parents and grandparents. Then we had to write what we wanted to impart to our own children regarding the other race. Finally we shared our answers with the group.

The responses were illuminating. Regarding their own race, everyone said they learned mostly positive characteristics with a few negative. That was certainly my case. The impressions I received were that most White people are capable, trustworthy, and leaders. That nothing is too difficult if we work hard, so expect to have plenty of opportunities, and take responsibility for them when they come. Advantage is ours to lose, not something we have to fight to earn. We can do anything we set our minds to.

Regarding members of the opposite race, everyone tended to have received either neutral or negative messages, such as they can't be trusted and they won't accept you. I grew in self-awareness through reflecting on my own answer! Most of the messages I received about Black people and my own whiteness had been implied, never explicitly stated. The truth was that we rarely talked about Black people. Many other White people said the same thing.

None of my African American brothers and sisters had that experience, however. None of them were able to go through their formative years without some kind of explicit conversation on the implications of race on their lives. For instance, my parents never had to talk to me about the dangers of "driving while Black." Yet this conversation seemed to be almost a rite of passage for teenage men and women of color.

For being part of the majority culture, I realized how easily I could insulate myself in my own racial bubble. As I pondered what had been imparted to me from my family, I had to recognize there was indeed a racial identity that had been taught to me. The danger comes when I lack self-awareness of these messages and the messages I receive about others. These positive messages about ourselves can quickly become a breeding ground for supremacy and arrogance, if I don't receive equally positive messages concerning those of other races.

Through awareness and self-reflection we can grow in ways that help us minimize racial insensitivity, and also offer the unique strengths and beauty of our own cultural identity, allowing the ability to also receive the unique strengths and beauty of others.

Each morning, most of us look at ourselves in the mirror. We check out our clothing, our hair, our makeup, or to make sure we didn't miss a spot shaving. We self-reflect. But only at a surface level. When it comes to our attitudes and behaviors regarding race, we don't self-reflect and evaluate ourselves enough and we don't often grant the right to others to evaluate us. We neglect to look into the proverbial mirror, perhaps for fear of what we might reflect or of what we've missed. As believers we have nothing to fear in self-reflection, however, because Christ is still sanctifying us out of our sinful selves and forming us into His likeness. There really is hope for each of us in Christ.

We also have nothing to fear in inviting others to tell us the truth about ourselves. We need trustworthy, honest, and compassionate believers around us who are willing to say hard things, even at the risk of hurting our feelings. When my (Josh's) best friend, Johnthan, saw a photo of me on social media, he immediately called me and said, "Clem, it is time to let the Lord continue to do His work in your life."

"What do you mean?"

"It's time to let your hair go! Your hairline has been receding and thinning, and now it's just painful to look at. I can't let my boy be out in these streets lookin' like that. It's time to let it go."

I thought, *I need a new best friend.* But that's just it: we must love each other enough to not allow us to be out in these streets looking crazy.

I regularly let Hazen know about himself, and he takes great pleasure in sharing my shortcomings as well. Relationship affords us this right and ability. We must hold a mirror up to each other so we can see our true selves. Though potentially taxing and daunting, there is no other path to reconciliation, except by way of deep and honest relationships.

INGREDIENT #2: TRUST

The foundation of every strong relationship is trust. Not just a general trust in a person's competency or word, or a trust that a person is who they presenting themselves to be. While those basic kinds of trust are necessary, the trust that allows for enduring reconciled relationships is the kind that forms when we believe a person is conducting themselves truly with our best interest in mind. The deep question of trust that most people ask is, "Are you for me, or for yourself?" If you communicate that you are *for someone* in the way you treat them, and then demonstrate that to be true over time, then you earn the kind of trust that builds enduring reconciled relationships. When you discern someone's care for you is merely self-interested, then you naturally trust them less.

Unfortunately, we cannot make other people become more trustworthy, but we can understand how to be trustworthy ourselves. When we cultivate trustworthiness in ourselves, that attracts other trustworthy people and draws out the best in people who are inspired by our example. Here are three basic steps in building trust as a reconciler.

Learn from People's Stories and Courageously Share Your Own

There is an old expression, "God gave you two ears and one mouth, so you should listen twice as much as you speak." Scripture expresses it this way: "Everyone should be quick to listen, slow to speak" (James 1:19 NIV). Foundational to building enduring reconciled relationships is our willingness to take the time to ask good questions and express genuine interest in the stories of others. Be inquisitive. Start with questions, such as: Where did you grow up? What is your family like? What are you passionate about?

Early on in Josh's and my friendship, we met regularly for lunch and shared the best and worst of our week. We got to know each other's stories, and during our most intensive seasons of daily working together, I had no closer confidant. Josh was always a great listener, not just sharing his own experiences, but always attentive and asking good questions in our conversations.

> When we go out of our way to serve others, we reinforce the foundational message that says, *I am for you.*

If you become that person who shows genuine interest in others, then you will be taking the first step of building trust quickly. You can show people you care about who they are and where they come from by offering the simple gift of listening well.

Add Value to People's Lives by Serving Them

Not long ago my wife had emergency back surgery for a herniated disk, which came at the tail end of a two-week bout of

COVID-19. She was in recovery for more than a month and a half. In that trying season, our church and OneRace family (including Josh and his wife, Kisha) stepped up and took care of *all* our meals for the entire recovery period. Though in my pride I wanted to take care of things myself, I honestly needed the help. And our children were grateful not to have to eat cereal three meals a day! Not only did they provide meals, they sacrificially served in other ways by driving our kids to and from school, checking in on us daily, and praying fervently for us.

When we go out of our way to serve others, we reinforce the foundational message that says, *I am for you*. It can be big service "projects," such as the ways our friends served us during my wife's recovery. But it can also be small services. One way I try to practice serving is to inquire of customer service persons (especially persons of color) how they are doing and try to affirm them. This lets them know I see them as a person, not just a means for me to get whatever commodity I need to consume. Usually I get more of people's personal stories than I intend, because people know intuitively that genuinely caring people are trustworthy.

Be Honest, Vulnerable, and Forthright

I (Hazen) was working with a younger African American brother, and we had developed a close friendship. When I feel affection for people, I tend to hug them, pat them on the back, and give out high fives. However, one day I made the mistake of patting him on the head without thinking about it. He came to me later and said my action made him feel patronized. Though he believed the best about me and knew it wasn't my intention, he also didn't want me to do that again. I felt embarrassed at my mistake, but appreciated his honest feedback. I trusted him more because he was able to kindly be honest with me about my mistake.

I heard a pastor once say that we need to live "with our roof off and our walls down." It means we are willing to have the hard conversations about our feelings, thoughts, and ideas, and hold them up for input and correction from those in our lives and from the Holy Spirit.

For people of color, this means showing up as our full selves. There is never a reason to reduce who we are for the sake of getting along well with our White siblings. Early in my journey, I (Josh) felt the pressure to acquiesce to White culture in my speech and lifestyle. Feeling an underlying pressure to reduce myself, I even denied parts of my own humanity to assimilate into majority culture. I was buying into a lie that told me I needed to go along to get along. I have friend who often says, "God can't bless who you pretend to be." The same is true of our racial relationships. God can't mend and heal those relationships if we don't bring our whole selves to bear with each other in every environment. The work of vulnerability for us is to be ourselves and embrace the beauty of who and how God has made us. Through God's grace, He has made us worthy to live a fully present life without excuse.

Sometimes our deepest places of wounding can be triggered by cultural events, for both minority and majority cultures. A police-involved shooting broadcast on social media, the passage of legislation that impacts minorities in some disproportionate way, or exposure to racist and hurtful words or actions by the media. Majority culture may feel misunderstood, ignorant, afraid, or uncertain in such moments. Minority cultures may feel misunderstood, oppressed, afraid, and uncertain for entirely different reasons.

When people observe you being honest, vulnerable, and forthright (with a healthy dose of humility mixed in), especially around difficult or unpleasant conversations involving race and culture, then they see that you are indeed trustworthy. We aren't talking about venting the offense, but about expressing honestly how something has impacted you. Even if the feelings are negative.

It is that willingness to expose ourselves and be known for who we truly are that lets people know we can be trusted with their authentic selves. It can be risky to open up and share, "When this happened, I felt . . ." But this kind of vulnerability is essential for every reconciled relationship.

INGREDIENT #3: PROXIMITY

I (Hazen) grew up around an equestrian community, in which riding horses was a fun and common activity. But it was also a place where I never interacted with a minority person. (I was thrilled in my friendship with Josh to discover that he too loved riding!) My upbringing and choice of activities created a gap that kept me exposed only to people like me. When my wife and I had children, we didn't want them to experience that same kind of gap. While our older daughter enjoys horseback riding, we also intentionally put her in environments where she builds relationships cross culturally.

We truly cannot know one another, and each other's stories without creating proximity. Only by getting into one another's physical spaces, and especially people from the majority, can we be challenged to show proper honor to one another. It helped our friendship that Josh and I lived within three miles of each other and worked out of the same church offices. It made it easier to be in each other's worlds and to get to know each other's families.

Increasingly the barrier of proximity has less to do with geography than it has in the past, because of how technology has allowed relationships and connection to thrive across borders and time zones. However, many have failed in creating a reconciled community because they were unwilling to close the physical proximity gap. This is the gap that exists when we live in different parts of the city, attend different schools, and participate in different activities that cause us to silo. Often people of color are already accustomed to making the effort to close the proximity gap by crossing over into majority dominated spaces; members of the majority culture by and large do this far less. When someone from the majority culture makes the effort to reciprocate and come into a person of color's "home space," this communicates value.

In planning our prayer meetings, we made it a nonnegotiable that we would host them in both majority White and majority Black churches. That way, each would not just enter the other's "spaces" but also enter into their hearts and submit to their leadership. When we invited African American churches to host, we always went to great lengths to express that we wanted their worship expression to shine through, and for their pastor to take the lead in facilitating the gathering. This communicated value and trust to our Black brothers and sisters who were hosting dozens of White leaders and their congregations (some of them for the first time).

These prayer meetings also allowed necessary conversations, such as why some have difficulty prioritizing their time and energy to attend and participate with siblings of color; and what message we send when we're willing only to participate in things we are comfortable with, never sacrificing our comfort for the ethnic other. These gatherings helped us hold up a mirror to each leader so he or she could see themselves and wrestle with power dynamics and other issues of race. Though this effort brought some conflict, it also brought great healing—something that never would have been possible without proximity.

The early church modeled this kind of proximity:

They devoted themselves to the apostles' teaching and to fellowship, to the breaking of bread and to prayer. Everyone was filled with awe at the many wonders and signs performed by the apostles. All the believers were together and had everything in common. . . . Every day they continued to meet together in the temple courts. They broke bread in their homes and ate together with glad and sincere hearts, praising God and enjoying the favor of all the people. And the Lord added to their number daily those who were being saved. (Acts 2:42–44, 46–47 NIV)

This vibrant and healthy community life resulted in the growth of the church and the witness of God's power in their midst. None of this would have been possible without living in proximity.

We won't truly be there to support and help one another if we aren't close enough at hand when challenges hit. Part of why my church and OneRace community could help when my wife had surgery was because of proximity. When we close the proximity gap, and get into community and relationships with those different from us, we take a vital step toward building enduring relationships as reconcilers.

INGREDIENT #4: INTENTIONALITY OVER TIME

Josh and I ran a half-marathon together. We ran it in 90-degree sweltering Atlanta heat. Josh may deny this, but we were both dying by the end. What gave us the endurance to finish was our encouragement to each other! Running a half-marathon doesn't just happen the day of the race. It requires lengthy and intentional training time and investment. It's the same with living as a reconciler. We must view relationships like a marathon, rather than a sprint. If we want to live truly reconciled, we can't only apply effort toward relationships seasonally.

On countless occasions we have heard minority pastors ruefully reflect that they get invitations to attend prayer gatherings or to come together for fellowship only when racial tragedies excite the conscience of the local White pastors and their congregations.

No one wants to feel like they are only thought of when their presence is in some way useful. Just as Paul tells Timothy to "be prepared in season and out of season" (2 Tim. 4:2 NIV), we must also be intentional about our relationships in every season of life and ministry.

The reality is that we will likely only have capacity for a few key relationships of the quality we have described in this chapter, so choose them wisely and do not neglect them. When we show endurance in our relationships with others, by consistently communicating, spending time together, and growing in authentic connection, then we will have deeply rewarding, mutually supportive reconciled friendships. Through consistency and endurance over time, we build powerful bonds that will have resilience even in the face of conflict. We never lightly cast aside something we have invested lots of time into. Through such efforts we begin to truly know the stories, which in turn help us create transforming relationships for both you and your brothers and sisters in Christ.

6

Own the Story through Personal Practices

While part of the desire for reconciliation ministry was birthed for me (Hazen) out of the absence of meaningful relationships with people of color growing up, it was actually a season of prayer that awakened in my heart a calling for reconciliation work. In 2007, when I was twenty-three years old, I set my heart to do a forty-day season of fasting and prayer. I started out pursuing God for transformation in my life and for an awakening in the church. On about day thirty, quite unexpectedly, God impressed clearly upon me a distinct assignment of reconciliation. From that time on, it has remained a key point of intercession for my life, for the church where I pastor, and for the movements I participate in.

Had I not engaged in prayer and fasting, I may have never heard that call. We can consume a lot of good information and still remain unchanged. To be reconcilers, the knowing comes through head knowledge, while the owning comes through the Holy Spirit's convicting and redeeming work in our hearts. He takes the knowledge we've gained and uses it to prepare us for the mission.

> Your own issues must be your primary area of responsibility, because that is the place where you can affect change the fastest.

I've found the best way to own our stories and to pursue reconciliation is to pursue the spiritual disciplines that draw us closer to God. The change we long to see in the world "out there" needs first to begin "in here," deep in the sanctuary of our own hearts.

FROM THE INSIDE OUT

In Matthew 7, Jesus told a parable in which He addressed the issue of judgment toward one another, using the metaphor of trying to help a friend dislodge something from his or her eyes:

> Why do you look at the speck of sawdust in your brother's eye and pay no attention to the plank in your own eye? How can you say to your brother, "Let me take the speck out of your eye," when all the time there is a plank in your own eye? You hypocrite, first take the plank out of your own eye, and then you will see clearly to remove the speck from your brother's eye. (Matt. 7:3–5 NIV)

Jesus noted that we always find it easier to try to help someone else with their problems rather than focus on our own. We can apply this idea to how we often address the social ill of racism, no matter our race. We are often eager to do so, leaving our own bigger problems unaddressed. And yet Jesus taught that we must deal with our own issues first. Your own issues must be your primary area of responsibility, because that is the place where you can affect change the fastest.

Note something else powerful in this parable. Jesus didn't say, "Leave the sawdust in your brother's eyes and just attend to yourself." He said, "*First*, take the plank out of your own eye, and then you will see clearly." This is why we must begin with *owning* the story—in which we examine and let God transform *our* hearts before we move to remedy the sickness of racism we find in others. If we don't begin with healing and transformation within us, we literally *can't see* to help those around us.

How do you begin to remove those planks? First, you need to submit to an eye exam. In my own journey, I (Hazen) found that asking good questions from friends of color is essential. Early on in our unity work, Josh and I began debriefing about our meetings with leaders in a way that allowed us to be both kind but honest. I had to trust Josh to tell me if I was coming on too strong, or not strong enough when discussing topics of justice, the gospel, and what it says about reconciliation. We need to be open to letting the Holy Spirit convict our hearts, and even show us things through those around us. His chosen instruments of examination are often the things that happen in everyday life and our closest relationships, all in the context of the body of Christ and the Word of God. Though it may not feel good in the moment, such exposures are God's greatest gift to us on our journeys of sanctification and reconciliation.

If you are open to God examining you in this way, you won't have to wait long or go far. Why not begin by praying this prayer and perhaps even reflecting on places where the previous chapters of this book have exposed pride, anger, pain, or defensiveness in your own heart?

> Blessed Trinity, Father, Son, and Holy Spirit,
>
> I believe You search me and know me through and through. You know every place in me that is not like Jesus. Make what You know about my shortcomings known to me.
>
> Please show me where I have strongholds of superiority about my race. Show me where I have blind spots in my love for others, and where through commission of sin or omission of righteousness, I have failed to reflect the perfection of Your kind, forgiving, merciful, humble love to the people around me.
>
> Heal my eyes of any planks, so I can truly see myself and those around me the way You do. Amen.

The Compelling Force Behind Our Spiritual Formation

The vision statement for OneRace that Josh and I once crafted said we were "teaching cities to love across color, class, and culture." I remember what came up in my heart as we wrestled with this language. *Was it specific enough concerning our movement's purpose? Was it overly idealistic? Was it cliché? Is love really the solution to overcoming racism?*

Perhaps you too have wrestled with skepticism regarding a "love is the answer" refrain, thinking, *Come on, we aren't going to solve generations of racial problems by holding hands and singing "Kumbaya."* But the kind of love we are talking about isn't that syrupy sweet, feel-good romanticized love.

Scripture tells us, "This is how we know what love is: Jesus Christ laid down his life for us. And we ought to lay down our lives for our brothers and sisters" (1 John 3:16 NIV). This kind of love is often referred to by those who write on spiritual formation as "cruciform love." This sacrificial love Christ displayed on the cross, the kind that cost the Son of God His life, is the love we are to emulate in our care for one another, and must be the cornerstone of our reconciliation work.

Too often we oversimplify and confuse the type of love we need to pursue as reconcilers, instead believing and/or pursuing the corrupted kind, which does little to effect reconciliation and allows for cynicism to set itself up in our hearts and minds. Here are three misrepresentations, in particular, we need to be aware of.

Hollywood's Definition of Love

One of the major influences to our corrupted view of love is the impact of our entertainment culture (music, movies, books) that has reduced the experience of "love" to an effervescent feeling, rather than a specific set of defined behaviors rooted in commitment to one another. Moreover, these "Hollywood" expressions of love are often narcissistic. They are selfishly motivated with personal satisfaction at the center rather than biblical love centered around care for the other.

Nowhere is the requirement to de-center ourselves in order to love more clearly stated than in the scriptural admonition to husbands: "Husbands, love your wives, just as Christ loved the church and gave himself up for her. . . . In this same way, husbands ought to love their wives *as their own bodies.* He who loves his wife loves himself. After all, *no one ever hated their own body,* but they feed and care for their body, just as Christ does the church" (Eph. 5:25, 28–29 NIV). That is the re-definition of love the gospel invites us into—to care for others more than we care for ourselves.

To love this way takes time, energy, and intentionality. It requires that we constantly re-orient ourselves to think about the needs of others. Lest we think this prioritization of others is only for those closest to us, Paul says, "Do nothing out of selfish ambition or vain conceit. Rather, in humility *value others above yourselves,* not looking to your own interests but *each of you to the interests of the others*" (Phil. 2:3–4 NIV). True biblical love puts others at the center of our consideration. In Paul's great discourse on love, he says succinctly that love "is not self-seeking" (1 Cor. 13:5 NIV). If the church embraces the radical demands of this kind of love for one another, there would be no room for prejudice or arrogance, because the selfishness, narcissism, and worship of one's race are contrary to the very nature of Christian love.

Meaningless Talk of Love

Another misrepresentation of love is the kind that gets talked about in our pulpits far more than we have actualized it in our communities. Paul says, "*The goal of this command is love,* which comes from a pure heart and a good conscience and a sincere faith. Some have departed from these and have turned to meaningless talk" (1 Tim. 1:5–6 NIV). John also discusses the act of love: "This is how we know what love is: Jesus Christ laid down his life for us. And *we ought to lay down our lives for our brothers and sisters.* If anyone has material possessions and sees a brother or sister in need but has no pity on them, how can the love of God be in that person? *Dear children, let us not love with words or speech but with actions and in truth*" (1 John 3:16–18 NIV).

Early on in my (Hazen) journey with reconciliation work, an African American pastor in our city, who has since become a good friend, shared with me his struggle in joining with our efforts. He said, "I have seen lots of reconciliation work where the backroom conversations didn't match the public declarations." This revelation pained my heart, and I committed on the spot to labor by God's grace to do better.

My friend didn't want to be part of a movement that was "loving in words" but not loving in "deed or truth." We don't want to either.

The "Good, Moral Behavior" of Love

Finally, we can become cynical about love because religious mentalities have reduced it to good, moral behavior, rather than to living passionately connected to God and His purposes. In His Upper Room Discourse, Jesus said that "whoever has my commands and keeps them, he it is who loves me" (John 14:21). If you take this statement out of context, it can certainly sound as though He is suggesting that obeying God (i.e., living by the moral principles enshrined in the Ten Commandments) is at the heart of loving God. Certainly, we should live morally, and the Ten Commandments provide good guidance for treating one another with honesty, fidelity, and uprightness. However, as Jesus makes clear in the previous chapter, He defines God's commands this way: "A new commandment I give to you, that you love one another: just as I have loved you, you also are to love one another" (John 13:34).

> We can't obey the law of Christ in love and say that other people's problems are not our own, even if their culture or class is far removed from us.

In His first public message, the Sermon on the Mount, Jesus gave what is known anecdotally as the Golden Rule: "Do to others as you would have them do to you" (Luke 6:31 NIV). But in His closing words to the disciples in the upper room on the night He was betrayed, Jesus upped the ante and called them not just to do what is morally right but to love one another as He loved them. Shortly after, He went to the cross to display what kind of love this statement intended.

FOLLOWING JESUS' MODEL OF LOVE

The sacrificial love Jesus modeled on the cross is undoubtedly at the core of His instruction to obey the commands of God. Jesus showed us that obedience to Him begins with sincere, selfless, heartfelt love for God and one another. Jesus' love is proactively just toward others, making their concerns His own.

Jesus came to "own the story" of our sin and brokenness, though He was without fault or sin. Likewise, we can't obey the law of Christ in love and say that other people's problems are not our own, even if their culture or class is far removed from us. Consider how far removed from our brokenness, sin, and the resulting problems Jesus was in heaven. Yet He came down and got right into our mess. And He invites us to do the same for one another.

Jesus modeled for us that real kingdom fruitfulness flows from a transformed heart of love, living out of connection to the Trinity. He didn't just teach that we love our enemies, persecutors, and betrayers; He embraced them at the heart level, washing the feet of Judas, healing the ear of a man who came to capture Him in the garden, and ultimately dying at His enemies' hands with parting words of forgiveness and mercy.

In this, we see that obeying Christ's commands must be more than a morality where we do not commit sin against one another (i.e., "I am not a racist!"), but that we take an active care for others that takes on the burdens of others as our own. As Paul wrote, "Walk in the way of love, just as Christ loved us and gave himself up for us as a fragrant offering and sacrifice to God" (Eph. 5:2 NIV). If we walk in the way of love, as Christ modeled, then we will constantly be "giving ourselves up" sacrificially. Which Paul described as a fragrance and an offering, a worshipful sacrifice that pleases God. The love Jesus expressed in this way changed the world. Reconciliation!

Reconciler, you must embrace the biblical imperative of Christian love as a means and end goal for your personal transformation and the transformation of your community, city, and nation. Remember that the quality of our Christianity is ultimately measured not by how much we know, but by how much that knowledge compels us to love God and others—to own the story. Jesus said it best: "By this all people will know that you are my disciples, if you have love for one another" (John 13:35).

Once we deeply embrace this as the catalyst and the ultimate goal of our transformation, then we can labor by God's grace in our practices to grow to *truly love as never before*.

SPIRITUAL PRACTICES THAT HELP US OWN THE STORY

As I (Hazen) shared earlier in this chapter the beginning of my journey toward becoming a racial reconciler, I recognized that owning the story came only by intentionally practicing spiritual disciplines. This is at the heart of reconciliation. We need the Holy Spirit's guidance.

Many books have been written on spiritual disciplines, but few address how those pursuing reconciliation ministry need to directly apply these practices to their own hearts and work. We are a movement committed to the discipleship of the Reconciler, not just the work of reconciliation in society at large. We are becoming the change we long to see, and that cannot happen if we don't first engage with God through spiritual practices.

Though we could look at many spiritual practices and their connection to reconciliation work, we're going to focus in this chapter on four disciplines (and in the next chapter, we're going to look at a few other disciplines as they apply to corporate life, though all spiritual disciplines apply to *both* individual and corporate practice).

LAYING A BIBLICAL FOUNDATION

Today many people, inside and outside the church, are espousing a wide variety of ideas on the subject of race. If we consume those ideas and regurgitate them without personally holding them up to God's Word, we can easily lose our scriptural moorings. The psalmist writes in Psalm 119:105, "Your word is a lamp to my feet and a light to my path." If you find yourself lost and stumbling around issues of race, your greatest resource is to acquaint yourself with what God's Word has to say on the subject. Let's remember the oft-quoted quality of the Berean character: "The Berean Jews were of more noble character than those in Thessalonica, for they received the message with great eagerness and *examined the Scriptures every day to see if what Paul said was true*" (Acts 17:11 NIV).

In an increasingly biblically illiterate generation, we cannot overly stress that we must prioritize Scripture in our lives. When presented with truths that on the surface seem self-evident, a good friend of mine says, "There is no confidence like biblical confidence." For the Christian reconciler, there is no substitute for any opinion, research study, or personal experience that should supersede the weight of God's Word in our lives. Though we can consider cultural, educational, and experiential inputs, it all must be submitted to the authority of God's Word, and forged in the furnace of community committed to doctrinally sound teaching.

I would have departed from the priority of reconciliation as a ministry imperative in my life many times, except that I have been so convinced of its importance to God by reading and meditating on His Word. What I see in Scripture—that reconciliation was a core element of Jesus' ministry—leaves me no alternative.

We must take time to understand what He has said to us in Scripture about reconciliation. We cannot afford to skip this step in our spiritual formation as reconcilers. When we become biblically persuaded and informed, we speak not just out of our own human conviction, but authoritatively and truthfully as God's representatives.

We recommend studying Scripture using a trusted commentary. Studying the relationship of Jew and Gentile in the first-century church is a fascinating place to start and be informed by the Word concerning race. Begin with Acts, but expand your study to examine the interactions of Jews, Samaritans, and Gentiles throughout the Gospels and as described in the epistles. It will change the way you understand the Bible and its message to us. So many issues we face today, we find paralleled in the first-century church. Our team with OneRace did a weekly Bible study where we read and discussed race in each chapter of the book of Acts. It was quite eye opening! Consider trying this with a friend or group of friends from a different culture.

Also get into the habit of going back and referencing your resources. When you consume a great resource on reconciliation, whether it be a class, book, or sermon, take time to read the context of the referenced Scriptures. As you do, you will find that they may speak to you outside what the teacher presents. You will get fresh insight, and you will be examining the Word of God for yourself!

As you engage in this spiritual discipline, you will undoubtedly experience conviction. The writer of Hebrews explained it this way, "The Word of God is alive and active. Sharper than any double-edged sword, it penetrates even to dividing soul and spirit, joints and marrow; it judges the thoughts and attitudes of the heart" (4:12 NIV).

All of us have thoughts and attitudes toward our brothers and sisters of different races or cultures that need to be addressed. Often, our biases and prejudices go undisturbed, running in the background like an operating system, causing us to react consciously or unconsciously in un-Christlike ways. Our ungodly mentalities go unchallenged until we are confronted with the sword of God's Word. Maybe the implications of a racist action fall upon a family member or loved one, and our lack of empathy or offense is stirred up. Perhaps we hit the lock button on our car doors when we come across someone of a different race walking by, and we think, *Why did I do that?* There we discover the truth: that we have wicked ways still residing in us.

Yet God is so kind! He makes a way for us to receive grace. The writer of Hebrews beckons us to "approach God's throne of grace with confidence, so that we may receive mercy and find grace to help us in our time of need" (4:16 NIV).

ENGAGING IN A PROGRESSION OF PRAYER

As we pray, we experience a progression that connects us to God's throne. First, we experience confidence that God is listening. That leads us to confession, which helps resolve our sin so that we might enter boldly. And then we freely make requests that God will intervene in challenging situations both big and small. Let's consider this progression, as it relates to us as reconcilers.

Confidence

All our unwillingness to begin and remain with prayer is rooted in misunderstanding the power of God's throne and our access to it. The more we know how powerful God is and simultaneously how welcome we are in His presence, the more quickly we will avail ourselves of the access Jesus' blood has purchased.

Imagine you were given the number to a direct phone line sitting on the president's desk in the Oval Office, and the president encouraged you to call whenever you needed something. Wouldn't that be action number one when you encountered some injustice beyond your power to remedy? Yet what you have been given is even more intimate access to the eternal sovereign Ruler of the universe, whose throne is the governmental epicenter of all creation. He has said, "Call Me and ask whenever you have a need, My child." This is quite a step above the Oval Office. We must remember that His help isn't secured by eloquent appeals of pretension but by simple faith-filled appeals of desperation. Jesus taught this principle in a story of a tax collector who went to the temple to pray: "God, have mercy on me, a sinner" (Luke 18:13 NIV).

The most powerful prayers are rooted in a guttural awareness of our brokenness and need for God's mercy. One of the greatest gifts we could receive as His church is for us to lose confidence in *our own* righteousness so that we can truly learn to pray with desperation and true humility. As Paul wrote, "Godly sorrow brings repentance that leads to salvation and leaves no regret, but worldly sorrow brings death" (2 Cor. 7:10 NIV).

We must recognize this truth regarding our race. I (Hazen) speak from experience that White guilt can be a painful and disqualifying experience, it can cause us to want to avoid the painful places of injustice even in the place of prayer. We don't want to carry the racial struggles or those of our culture before God, because we feel so ashamed of our sin. Despite this, we must believe God's Word over our own experience of guilt, shame, anger, or despair. Even in our brokenness, we are beckoned to come, that we might confess and be made clean.

Confession

The apostle John noted our tendency to justify ourselves: "If we say we have no sin, we deceive ourselves, and the truth is not in us" (1 John 1:8). We must stop saying we don't have attitudes that aren't at times sinfully superior, preferential, biased, prejudicial, or racist. We *all* do in our broken humanity. What distinguishes the reconciler on a transformative journey is not that they don't have sin with regard to race, but that they possess the ability to, without shame, acknowledge that they do, and bring it to God for healing! John kindly reminded us that the true remedy for our sins is not denial but confession: "If we confess our sins, he is faithful and just to forgive us our sins and to cleanse us from all unrighteousness" (1 John 1:9).

Our transgression has often been committed with intentionality, and its acknowledgment and renunciation require similar intentionality. As you confront your sin, remind yourself, "Saying that He is faithful means that He forgives me every time. And saying He is just in forgiving is true because He has already paid the price for me to receive mercy."

Reconciler, let's acknowledge our sins and then make our way boldly to God's throne so we can change the world with our prayers! I (Hazen) will often begin times of prayer acknowledging my need for God's conviction, and then take time to quietly pay attention with an open heart to the Holy Spirit's leading. More often than not, a Bible verse or a situation might come to mind that serves as a prompt for confession. Rather than being overly introspective during these times, believe in simple faith for God to do by the Spirit what He has promised in John 16:8: "When he [the Holy Spirit] comes, he will convict the world concerning sin."

We can trust furthermore that if the Holy Spirit impresses nothing on our hearts, we are released to move on in our prayers. But we start first by asking God, "Search me, God, and know my heart; test me and know my anxious thoughts. See if there is any offensive way in me, and lead me in the way everlasting" (Ps. 139:23–24 NIV).

Supplication

Having taken time to enter before God with confidence, having made confession, we are free to move into supplication. A great way to lift our vision is to organize a prayer list that stretches us to believe God for things greater than our own immediate needs. Try praying for needs based on concentric circles of influence, first asking God to help yourself and your immediate family, next your extended family and friends, then your church community, city, nation, and finally, the nations of the earth. Combine your Bible study practice by praying God's Word back to Him. Pick out Bible passages—such as Psalm 33, Romans 15:13, and Colossians 1:9—and issues to carry before God at each level and regularly pray for each category. You may even feel God leading you into seasons of fasting as you pray for unity in the church, a gospel witness in your city, and for strength and righteousness among believers of all races.

I (Hazen) wear a simple red band every day on my right wrist, which has OneRace's key verses on it (John 17:21 and Acts 17:26). That band reminds me to pray those verses over my church and city.

PURSUING REPENTANCE

While many people think confession is the same as repentance, they are distinct, though inextricably linked. Confession is the act of recognizing you are wrong and a change of course is needed. Repentance is turning around and going in the right direction. True confession leads to accompanying repentance. Not to cut the distinction too finely, but often the practice of confession is engaged through our emotions in prayer with God and conversation with others, involving the sincere acknowledgment of sin. Meanwhile, repentance involves engaging our minds and wills to do differently moving forward.

If the heart is not softened and prepared for repentance by carrying our sins before God in confession, we will try to solve the problem in our own self-effort rather than through God's empowering grace. (Also connected is the practice of lament, which we will discuss in the next chapter.) As the unique steps in a dance complete the entire elegant movement, so confession, repentance, and lament build upon one another to form a series of practices that cultivate a heart of contrition that pleases God.

Real repentance involves resolving to take steps toward new behaviors. There are probably unconscious ways you have ungodly preferences for your own race and culture. It is not enough to become aware of this and confess it. You also need to begin to untangle the thought habits, impulses, and biases at the root of your racial partiality.

One area where this is true of me (Hazen) is in my *take charge* mentality. I have struggled with often trying to guide a conversation or action in the direction I think it needs to go, regardless of whether or not that is my job. In doing so, I neglect to value the leadership skills and opinions of others. I have found that this tendency is tied to my being a well-educated, affluent, White male, with a leadership gift and an outgoing personality. Certainly, all those things contribute, but it doesn't make that impulse holy or entirely wicked. So who can help me sort this out? Only the Holy Spirit. When I take questions to the Word and prayer, I discover that my desire to be helpful is being perverted by my assumption that I need to take charge, as if I am God's gift to the team. Take note, the unraveling of this mentality had to start with genuine awareness and confession—first that my arrogance was wrong and then that my repentance needed to instill within me a desire to be quick to listen and slow to speak, to ask questions before posing solutions, and to ask if my input is wanted before assuming it is needed. Am I fully healed of this vulnerability? Certainly not, but I have come a long way. Undoubtedly, these efforts at true repentance have made me a better leader, but most importantly a better Christian. In this space, I find myself being conformed to the humility, meekness, and gentleness I see in Jesus, a Person who always knew the right answer in every situation yet often started His conversations with a question.

Consider an area you know God has been inviting you to engage in with greater humility and accountability. Ask yourself, "What concrete steps can I take to respond to God's invitation?" And let God lead you into repentance.

CULTIVATING FORGIVENESS

Myra Thompson was the teacher of the Wednesday night Bible study that met each week at Emanuel AME Church in Charleston, South Carolina. On June 17, 2015, as they were finishing up their time together in prayer, twenty-one-year-old White supremacist Dylann Roof, bent on starting a race war, entered the sanctuary and shot and killed nine people. He shot Myra eight times. Upon his capture, Dylann expressed no remorse, telling FBI agents that, given the opportunity, he would do it again.

At his children's urging, Anthony Thompson, Myra's husband, reluctantly attended the bond hearing for his wife's murderer. Though he did not plan to say anything, when given the opportunity, he felt the Holy Spirit urge him to rise and offer words of forgiveness. Anthony called Dylann to repentance of his sins and salvation through Christ. While a profound and moving moment, this is not the most striking about Anthony's forgiveness. Three times a day, Anthony prays for Dylann's salvation and has written him letters continuing to pursue the well-being of the man who stole his wife's life.[1]

Anthony had not just modeled Jesus' forgiveness in a moment, he was living a daily practice of forgiving and blessing his enemies. Anthony's example brings new life to the Scripture that tells us to "love your enemies and pray for those who persecute you" (Matt. 5:44).

We may never be faced with offering the kind of sacrificial forgiveness that Anthony was faced with (we pray we never are). But we each still carry wounds from racial injustices and misunderstandings that affect our relationships. As reconcilers, we follow in the footsteps of Jesus, who bore the sin of the world, and we offer forgiveness and work to cultivate an environment in our lives, church, and community that willingly offers forgiveness through the grace of God.

7

Own the Story through Corporate Practices

During the summer of 2006, I (Hazen) was working with middle-school-aged kids at a summer camp in Texas. I had just begun serving the Lord in earnest the year before, and was zealous to see young people touched by God and get born again. In that season I stumbled across a verse in which God described the remedy for healing and reviving a backsliding nation. Though I didn't realize 2 Chronicles 7:14 is a fairly common revival Scripture, I was captivated by its possibilities.

What would it look like for healing to break forth in our land? The verse's promise corresponded to a deep longing in my heart to see God move dramatically in my own life. So I wrote the reference with a permanent marker on my camp staff backpack and carried it around with me all summer, praying for God to give me a spirit of humility and holiness, so healing could be released through my life to those around me.

The context is following the dedication of Solomon's Temple, a dramatic moment a generation in the making. After Solomon's prayer of dedication, literal fire filled the temple and God's glory was so substantial that the priests could not stand to minister (see 2 Chron. 5:14). God visited Solomon that night and gave him the ominous warning that though God's glory was among His people that day, a time was coming when the people would depart from His ways. In that season Israel would find restoration only by following God's prescription. God declared, "If my people who are called by my name humble themselves, and pray and seek my face and turn from their wicked ways, then I will hear from heaven and will forgive their sin and heal their land" (2 Chron. 7:14).

As I prayed this passage that summer, I saw dramatic spiritual growth and transformation. I was healed of several areas of personal sin struggle, and had a hunger for God unlike anything I had experienced before. The verse has since evolved into a life message for me, and in it are hidden precious truths for healing and blessing a diseased people. And though at the time, I focused on it in my personal life, it really is a prescription for corporate practice.

Undoubtedly we see that one of our greatest ailments historically and presently is racism in the church and in our society at large. And God is calling us today to join together in some spiritual disciplines that can be applied as a balm to the sickness of racism and division, and to heal our church and our country.

ENGAGING A KINGDOM OF PRIESTS

If we break down the passage, we can see four distinct areas of spiritual practice that allow us to corporately "own the story."

First, we pursue unity. Second, we offer contrition. Third, we present expressions of worship and intercession as a priestly people. Fourth, we identify and repent of the sins of the past and across our generations through a broken heart of lament.

These practices—which we can and must engage with personally as well—prepare first our own hearts, and then our collective hearts to live as reconcilers within reconciled communities. We will never deeply experience in a consistent way publicly what we do not practice privately. Furthermore, it is these corporate spiritual practices that prepare churches to bring transformative change in their communities. We must own the story within our churches, so we can change the story in our communities.

Through these corporate spiritual practices, we act as reconciling priests before God. Remember the worshipful cry of the multitude from all nations that John saw before the throne in heaven:

> They sang a new song, saying: "You are worthy to take the scroll and to open its seals, because you were slain, and with your blood you purchased for God persons from every tribe and language and people and nation. You have made them to be a kingdom and priests to serve our God, and they will reign on the earth." (Rev. 5:9–10 NIV)

Those in this multiethnic picture of the church in worship understood their identity was as a kingdom of priests! We don't need to wait until heaven to express that identity as a *united* kingdom made up of a diversity of priestly people from all nations, ethnicities, and cultures. We are that priesthood today, so let's discuss how to become like this heavenly vision in both heart and practice.

"IF MY PEOPLE WHO ARE CALLED BY MY NAME"

When Josh and I were engaged in the evangelistic outreach in which I served as prayer coordinator in 2015, I was in a time of prayer in my home office when I had a profound experience. I sensed the Holy Spirit speak to my heart that the movement of salvation I longed to see in our city wouldn't come until the racial divisions within the church were addressed. What God was showing me in a personal way during prayer, I came to discover was a truth that was being shouted from Scripture. An essential unity is implied in 2 Chronicles 7:14 when God said, "If my people who are called by my name." It isn't the dispersed factions of a divided church that have the power to minister healing to a nation, it is only when we come together under the banner of His name with a united purpose to pray and seek Him.

In Psalm 133, as well, we see a vivid description of the requirement of unity in invoking God's blessing: "How good and pleasant it is when God's people live together in unity!" (Ps. 133:1 NIV). The psalmist David went on to use two powerful metaphors to describe the power of unity: oil and dew. He declared, "It is like precious oil poured on the head, running down on the beard, running down on Aaron's beard, down on the collar of his robe" (v. 2 NIV). Imagine the high priest with oil flowing down his head, as a sign that he was going before God to minister on behalf of the people. This was not just any oil, but the fragrant consecrating oil that made the priest fit to stand before God. It represented his dedication to his ministry and his spiritual preparedness to serve God as a holy minister.

> God uniquely responds to the corporate unity of the body of Christ in ways that He does not necessarily respond to with individuals.

In the next verse, David declared the people of God dwelling in unity was "as if the dew of Hermon were falling on Mount Zion. For there the LORD bestows his blessing, even *life forevermore*" (NIV). Mount Hermon is the highest mountain in the north of Israel. Its "dew" would condense and come upon the tops of the hills of Palestine as a refreshing mist that would water and make green the flora of the arid region. The dew brings life and vitality to the dry, barren places.

What is a priest without oil? Unprepared to come into God's presence. What are the mountains without the dew? They would be dry, dusty, and devoid of life. We see in both pictures the beauty, consecration, and vitality that come upon a people "dwelling in unity."

Conversely picture the absence of such unity. The priest is unfit to serve; the land stricken and parched. So where unity exists, God's commanded blessing is evidenced as "life forevermore." So the prescription for a nation that is lifeless and defiled is that God's priestly people must place upon themselves the oil of unity and receive the refreshing of oneness, like dew upon the mountains or oil upon the head. The prescription for a divided and heartsick nation must start with a united church, "dwelling in unity" with one another. God's blessing of eternal life and salvation will advance under such conditions. That is His sure promise.

As these passages demonstrate, God uniquely responds to the corporate unity of the body of Christ in ways that He does not necessarily respond to with individuals. He stated to Solomon, "If my people . . ." He spoke in the plural, declaring that our united efforts do something distinct in God's heart. It is not the unbeliever or a society that ultimately has the spiritual responsibility to "own the story." It is the church together who will act as God's representatives on the earth. However, we cannot stop at being unified, for a united people must together take collective spiritual action to "own the story."

This is not to say we must strive for the corporate expression of spiritual ownership over our personal practices. If we do that, we have it all backward, because as we have already said, one builds upon the other so that the public witness of the church embodies the secret life of the believers as we practice from our individual "prayer closets." As we saw in the last chapter, a life prepared in the Word, prayer, confession, repentance, and forgiveness is ready to take ownership of personal and historical sins of the church and nation.

Spiritually prepared people living in community and moving in unity toward reconciliation are no small matters. We will see in the history of Israel such prepared people were the hinges on which the doors of national renewal and revival swung open (such as Ezra, Nehemiah, Esther, and Daniel). Thus it is essential not just to the church, but to the life of our nation that a corporate people learn to pray, seek God's face, humble themselves, and collectively turn from their "wicked ways." In doing so we will embrace the righteousness of God in a new and deeper way, together.

Reconciler, you play an important part of being such people. Having laid the foundations through your individual practice, now you can begin to deepen the spiritual "owning" of the story to the Christian community you participate in. This is how we move together as a united people, called by His name.

"HUMBLE THEMSELVES"

When we went to worship and intercede at the top of Stone Mountain in 2018, we focused on a segment of prayer called, "Who can ascend?" based on Psalm 24, which reads in part:

"Who may ascend the mountain of the LORD? Who may stand in his holy place? The one who has clean hands and a pure heart, who does not trust in an idol or swear by a false god" (vv. 3–4 NIV). Based on this verse OneRace invited hundreds of church leaders and thousands of young adults to gather at the spiritual high place over our city where the Ku Klux Klan was rebirthed in 1915 by a pastor in a ritual act of idolatry wearing all the counterfeit vestments of a priest.

After forty days of fasting and dozens of regional prayer meetings across the Atlanta area, we arrived in the opposite spirit, renouncing the idolatry and proclaiming reconciliation and revival over our city. That day, through humbling ourselves before God in confession and repentance, we truly believe through our intercession we opened a door for greater kingdom transformation. This would have not been possible if our hearts had not been prepared in consecration before God.

Consecration is not just meant to be individual, but involves the whole body coming into agreement with righteousness and out of agreement regarding the darkness of sin. When we do this, then our intercession and fasting can impact the spiritual realm in powerful ways that grant the church victory.

> In order to wield our weapons of "divine power," we must exercise that authority from a place of humility and consecration.

As we move forward in unity, we must humbly consider that the first responsibility of a priestly people is that we be set apart as holy. This becomes ever more important as we consider the element of spiritual conflict we engage in in the midst of doing the work of reconciliation. There is a kingdom of darkness and spiritual powers that want to stir up strife, conflict, and accusation, and to do as much destruction as they can to those who bear God's image. Jesus warned that "The thief comes only to steal and kill and destroy" (John 10:10). And Paul spoke of our need to be prepared in spiritual conflict saying, "Our struggle is not against flesh and blood, but against the rulers, against the authorities, against the powers of this dark world and against the spiritual forces of evil in the heavenly realms" (Eph. 6:12 NIV).

No power on earth is greater than God's consecrated people in united prayer. The church has been given authority in Christ over these hosts of wickedness, so we must be certain that we do not call "good evil and evil good" (see Isa. 5:20), otherwise we will not know where to make our stand. Paul spoke of our spiritual weapons, explaining that "though we live in the world, we do not wage war as the world does. The weapons we fight with are not the weapons of the world. On the contrary, they have divine power to demolish strongholds" (2 Cor. 10:3–4 NIV). Yet in order to wield our weapons of "divine power," we must exercise that authority from a place of humility and consecration, having rejected the influence of sin in which the kingdom of darkness traffics. In particular, the community of reconcilers must be free from pride, racism, prejudice, partiality, bitterness, anger, hatred, and unforgiveness. Only then are we empowered to deploy the weapons of our warfare with wisdom and spiritual effectiveness.

Often we want to resist the devil without first submitting ourselves in humility to God. When through confession and the resolution to walk out repentance we cleanse our hearts (inward motivations) and hands (outward actions), we are prepared to draw near to God as a priestly people on behalf of a world under the darkness and sway of the evil one.

"PRAY AND SEEK MY FACE"

In this verse we see that it isn't just intercessory prayer that God desires, it is also that we seek His face. Of course we seek His face through many aspects of the Christian life being directed toward knowing and engaging intimately with God. But as we consider how it connects corporately, we see that God is calling us to *worship* Him.

Jesus described the burning desire for reconciled worship that is in God's heart when He met with the Samaritan woman at the well in John 4. The woman came to the well alone to draw water, likely because her many husbands and her current immoral relationship had left her ostracized among her own community. Additionally, she was a Samaritan, which made her unclean. The Jews despised Samaritans as a "half-breed" people, as they were the descendants of the ten northern tribes of Israel who intermarried with Gentiles, following the conquest of Assyria. Therefore they were racially, religiously, and culturally abhorrent to the Jewish people.

Yet Jesus boldly crossed those lines to reach the heart of a woman He recognized as thirsty for God. His willingness to engage with her surprised even her, as she exclaimed, "How is it that you, a Jew, ask for a drink from me, a woman of Samaria? (For Jews have no dealings with Samaritans)" (John 4:9).

He responds by letting her know that a time of unity is coming: "A time is coming and has now come when the true worshipers will worship the Father in the Spirit and in truth, for they are the kind of worshipers the Father seeks" (v. 23 NIV). The cultural distinctions that had divided the nations were about to be abolished with the coming of a new covenant. Jesus was telling this woman, who had experienced rejection, broken relationships, and inferior status, that God desired her worship! Jesus would ultimately give His life to secure it. This is still what God is searching for today—a thirsty people who will worship Him in Spirit and in truth, seeking His face above all else.

Our worship is not meant to be expressed only within our individual denominational or cultural camps. Worship satisfies the heart of God when it comes together across those lines, for these "are the kind of worshipers the Father seeks."

On Juneteenth 2020, in the midst of the COVID-19 pandemic, more than twelve thousand believers from more than seven hundred churches gathered at Centennial Olympic Park to worship, pray, and protest in the heart of our city for a "March on Atlanta." From there we proceeded to march to our State Capitol building to proclaim that Jesus and His church care about racial justice. In the wake of the George Floyd death (and the tragic deaths of several other people of color), we felt impressed in this unique moment to call the church to seek God's face, to pray, and to speak up for reconciliation and justice. Thousands of believers marched down Martin Luther King Boulevard, their mouths filled with prayer and proclamations of righteousness and justice. While we wanted to make a clear statement to our city and nation, more importantly, we wanted our prayer and worship to be a statement from a *united church* before God that we care about what moves His heart. This agreement in prayer and worship is what moves the heart of our Father, who desperately wants His children to love and to speak up for one another across color, class, and culture.

When a united and consecrated church comes to God in humility, our worship and corporate prayers of agreement unlock powerful spiritual realities that literally cause angels and demons to move in the spiritual realm. In worship we agree regarding who God is, and in prayer we agree around what we desire Him to do. Thousands and thousands of things are set in motion when God's people come together in agreement to worship our Father in Spirit and in truth.

"TURN FROM THEIR WICKED WAYS"

When we glimpse through seeking His face how holy and righteous God is, we quake in comparison to how broken and sinful we are. Worship leads us into corporate repentance and lament—the ability to deeply identify and "own" our collective sins and those of the preceding generations. We find the idea of a solemn assembly of fasting, prayer, and repentance in Joel 2:12–17:

> "Even now," declares the LORD, "return to me with all your heart, *with fasting and weeping and mourning."*
>
> Rend your heart and not your garments. Return to the LORD your God, for he is gracious and compassionate, slow to anger and abounding in love, and he relents from sending calamity. Who knows? He may turn and relent and leave behind a blessing— grain offerings and drink offerings for the LORD your God.
>
> Blow the trumpet in Zion, *declare a holy fast, call a sacred assembly. Gather the people, consecrate the assembly*; bring together the elders, gather the children, those nursing at the breast. Let the bridegroom leave his room and the bride her chamber. Let the priests, who minister before the LORD, *weep between the portico and the altar.* Let them say, "Spare your people, LORD. Do not make your inheritance an object of scorn, a byword among the nations. Why should they say among the peoples, 'Where is their God?'" (Joel 2:12–17 NIV)

The context of this passage from Joel is a national economic crisis in which four successive locust plagues decimated the crops, destroying the agrarian-based economy. Even worse, Joel was prophesying that the locust plagues foreshadowed the imminent invasion of a foreign army as judgment. In light of these national crises, God called the people to gather united to humble and consecrate themselves and to cry out to God in intercession, with sincerity, repenting of the sins that brought judgment upon the land. It is this kind of corporate wholehearted return to the Lord that God instructs us to in the 2 Chronicles passage, to "turn from their wicked ways."

What began as confession and genuine repentance in the "rending of the heart" in verse 13 must mature to full corporate lamentation on behalf of the nation in verse 17, as priests were instructed to weep between the porch and the altar and to cry out for God to spare the nation of His judgment.

Sadly, Israel failed to heed God's warning to turn from wickedness. So the comparatively minor discipline of the locusts increased in severity and became the national crisis of the Babylonian captivity. A captivity they would only be released from through the intercession and lament of a righteous remnant after seventy years of bondage.

We see this lament in the life of Daniel most clearly in the intercessory prayer he made on behalf of his nation to be released from Babylonian exile. He recorded:

> I turned to the Lord God and pleaded with him in prayer and petition, in fasting, and in sackcloth and ashes.
>
> I prayed to the LORD my God and confessed: "Lord, the great and awesome God, who keeps his covenant of love with those who love him and keep his commandments, *we* have sinned and done wrong. *We* have been wicked and have rebelled; *we* have turned away from your commands and laws. *We* have not listened to your servants the prophets, who spoke in your name to our kings, our princes and our ancestors, and to all the people of the land. . . .

We and our kings, our princes and our ancestors are
covered with shame, LORD, because *we* have sinned against
you. (Dan. 9:3–6, 8 NIV)

Note the genuine contrition displayed through fasting, sack-
cloth, and ashes. This was not just a moment of lament, but appears
to be a period lasting hours or perhaps days. As Daniel entered
into his prayer, he "owned" the story of his people and their past—
telling the Lord that "*we* have" done things against God, not that
"they" did those things.

None of us would fault Daniel for being resentful of the generation that preceded him. It was their disobedience that brought
the judgment that resulted in his being taken to Babylon as a
young captive boy. The sins that landed Israel in Babylonian captivity were not his own, nor even those of his own generation.
The testimony of Daniel, even among his enemies in his old age,
was that "they could find no ground for complaint or any fault,
because he was faithful, and no error or fault was found in him"
(Dan. 6:4). Yet he emphatically declared ownership of the sins on
behalf of the people, saying over and over, "We . . ." He identified
with the disobedience of his people as though it were his own,
because in a very real sense, that was how Daniel saw it.

He concluded his prayer beseeching God with all his heart:
"Lord, listen! Lord, forgive! Lord, hear and act! For your sake, my
God, do not delay, because your city and your people bear your
Name" (Dan. 9:19 NIV).

Daniel's genuine intercession, repentance, and lament moved
the heart of God and attracted God's favor, as an angel was sent
speedily with news of God's plan for Israel (Dan. 9:20–23). The
angel Gabriel greeted Daniel by telling him, "You are highly esteemed" (Dan. 9:23 NIV). Oh, that we would humble ourselves

and fast, pray, and lament in such a way as to be esteemed by God!

If we will "own" our story, as Daniel did with sincerity, rending our heart before God in fasting, prayer, repentance, and lament, we will stir the heart of God to act. He is the only one who can bring us out of bondage to the oppressive systems of every earthly "Babylon."

Daniel's example of lament was one of the theme passages around the "Day of Remembrance," a multisite event in churches across Atlanta on the Sunday of the four hundredth anniversary of the first enslaved peoples to North America. During the event, participants learned of the past four centuries and walked through a liturgy of lament, calling congregations to know, own, and change the story. Church altar spaces were filled with people lamenting the collective sins of our nation, just as Daniel had. A family member of mine (Hazen) attended one of the services not far from her house. Following the event, she told me that when she responded to the invitation to enter into lament, something broke in her heart for the first time and she wept over the racial sins of our nation. These kinds of pure offerings of contrition are what turn back the collective judgment of sin for our transgression, and what evoke God's blessing on the church and our nation.

We see the power of Daniel's intercession, this righteous servant of old when he owned the collective story of his people as his own. Let us take heart that God promises the same restoration to His church when we turn from our "wicked ways" and turn toward Him. "Draw near to God, and he will draw near to you," James tells us. "Cleanse your hands you sinners, and purify your hearts, you double-minded. Be wretched and mourn and weep. Let your laughter be turned to mourning and your joy to gloom. Humble yourselves in the presence of the Lord, and he will exalt you" (James 4:8–10). This New Testament picture of corporate repentance and lament has an attached promise: that if we humble ourselves in this way, God will exalt us.

GOD'S RESPONSE TO US

The final part of 2 Chronicles 7:14 shows us the remedy to the illness of racism within our nation. God promises: "I will hear from heaven and will forgive their sin and heal their land." If we will unite as a people, humble ourselves through consecration, seek God's face in worship and prayer, and turn from wickedness with a heart of lament, God will respond. He will hear. He will forgive. And He will heal.

God's hearing is not a general one, as in the same way we would hear but then choose to ignore a person's request. This hearing implies a responsiveness to our cries, that because we are heard, God will act on our behalf. John explains that promise in 1 John 5:15: "If we know that he hears us in whatever we ask, we know that we have the requests that we have asked of him."

God's forgiveness implies both our sins' removal from the ledger as well as the diminishing of their consequences. As He says to those in Isaiah's day, "'Come now, let us settle the matter,' says the LORD. 'Though your sins are like scarlet, they shall be as white as snow; though they are red as crimson, they shall be like wool. If you are willing and obedient, you will eat the good things of the land'" (Isa. 1:18–19 NIV).

And the third promise God offers is that He will heal the land, meaning not only is God responding to help us spiritually by removing our sin, He is also restoring in society what has been sick and broken because of sin. We see in our nation a declining participation in church, rising atheism, unprecedented chemical and sexual addiction, and a mental health crisis of anxiety and depression. This is the sickly state of our culture, and in some cases of the church as well. We are desperately in need of reformation and revival. But we believe one of the primary hindrances that allows sin to continue to fester like an open sore is that the church has refused to unite and truly own the great national sin of racism, hatred, White supremacy, and its ripple effects.

Yet we have hope. We have seen the Spirit moving through the hearts and minds of thousands who have taken this message to heart, who are owning the story, and who are seeking God in fasting, prayer, worship, corporate repentance, and lament. Their commitment is for us to receive revival through a reconciled and united church, one who is spiritually ready to take on the task of "changing the story" for generations to come.

8

Own the Story through Cultural Humility

Conflict is how I would describe the early days of my relationship with Hazen. And if I'm honest, we still have a considerable amount of interpersonal and racial conflict. We've just learned to handle it better. Some ignorance. Some bias. Such is the nature of reconciliation work. The very name means to put back together again or to restore harmony. This means that disruption has taken place, and if the past is any indicator, disruption will take place into the future.

Hazen and I wouldn't be worth our salt if we didn't wrestle through this stuff personally and together. Once I told Hazen, "I don't need your blue-eyed and blond-haired conclusion."

Hazen responded, "My eyes aren't blue and my hair isn't blond. That statement was steeped in racial bias."

He was right.

And Hazen once made a blanket statement about the Black church that was steeped in caricatures. I had to confront him over it. Truth and humility have been the glue that has made our relationship and work stick together. It is the very substance of reconciliation.

Hazen and I learned early that we would either fight each other or fight to be one. We chose the latter. This took tremendous consideration, hard work, many tough conversations, and lots of humility. Though we haven't gotten it right every time, we have fought to be faithful to Christ in our relationship and to operate with cultural humility. Our dynamic reminds me much of Paul and Peter's relationship.

These leaders of the early church loved the gospel and undoubtedly loved each other. Yet we also see that they didn't always get it right either, and that they needed rebuke and reconciliation as well. They needed to own the story and exhibit cultural humility. Something we all need to do if we want to be successful reconcilers.

PAUL, PETER, AND RACISM

The apostles Peter and Paul are profound figures in Christianity and central to the gospel movement. They are giants in the faith. Peter walked intimately with Jesus. Paul experienced Jesus' visitation, radically saving him. In Matthew 14, Peter walked on water as Jesus bid him to come. Paul's scholarly gift under the power of the Holy Spirit led him to pen thirteen letters that would go on to be canonized. In Matthew 16, Peter was the one who acknowledged Jesus as the Christ for the very first time. Paul worked diligently spreading the gospel, despite his persecution, arrest, imprisonment, and later execution.

Yet we too see that Peter's role was complex. A Jew, Peter focused on sharing the gospel with other Jews. But in Acts 10, we see God expand Peter's ministry focus when Peter received a heavenly vision about the inclusion of Gentiles in the family of God. Peter told the other believers: "You are well aware that it is against our law for a Jew to associate with or visit a Gentile. But God has shown me that I should not call anyone impure or unclean" (v. 28 NIV). A few verses later he stated: "Truly I understand that God shows no partiality, but in every nation anyone who fears him and does what is right is acceptable to him" (vv. 34–35).

Peter was clear about God's intentions among the nations: He desires to save even the Gentiles and include them in God's grand narrative. By the time Peter arrived in Galatia, however, he appeared to be conflicted and even willing to compromise on this revelation:

> When Cephas [Peter] came to Antioch, I [Paul] opposed him to his face, because he stood condemned. For before certain men came from James, he was eating with the Gentiles; but when they came he drew back and separated himself, fearing the circumcision party. And the rest of the Jews acted hypocritically along with him, so that even Barnabas was led astray by their hypocrisy. But when I saw that their conduct was not in step with the truth of the gospel, I said to Cephas before them all, "If you, though a Jew, live like a Gentile and not like a Jew, how can you force the Gentiles to live like Jews?" (Gal. 2:11–14)

Peter presented as if the Gentiles were good enough to be proselytized but not good enough to be part of the family. How did such a thing happen? And how did it get resolved?

Conflict Stemming from the Past

When Peter allowed his ethnic pride to undermine the gospel unity's, his actions became detrimental to the expansion of the gospel. Tim Keller described the situation well:

> Racial pride must have entered into it. It had been drilled into Peter, and all the Jews, since their youth that Gentiles were "unclean." While hiding beneath the facade of religious observance, Peter and other Jewish Christians were probably still feeling disdain for Christians from "inferior" national and racial backgrounds. Peter was allowing cultural differences to become more important than gospel unity.[1]

It is important that we understand the dynamic and history between the Jews and the Gentiles. For centuries they existed under an abiding tension. The Jews felt in every way superior to the Gentiles, namely because of their religious piety and their relationship with Yahweh. A popular Jewish prayer from the period said simply, "Blessed are you O God, King of the Universe, Who has not made me a Gentile."[2]

The Gentiles repaid the Jews' spiritual smugness with resentment and exclusion.[3]

Hypocrisy in Reaction

A group from James—the church in Jerusalem—arrived, and Peter began to distance himself from the Gentile believers. He refused to share in meals or communion with the Gentiles presumably because of what the Jewish believers might have thought. It was easier for Peter to withdraw from fellowship with the Gentile believers than to stand against potential peer pressure and internal conflict. Instead he bowed to the whims of people pleasing, ethnocentrism, and/or a lack of conviction. In other words, he acted as a moderate.

It was bad enough that Peter's decision to cower under pressure and retreat called his credibility into question, but worse, it led others astray: "The rest of the Jews acted hypocritically along with him, so that even Barnabas was led astray by their hypocrisy" (Gal. 2:13). His decision led the whole group into deception.[4]

Peter had a grand opportunity to lead the Jewish believers into a greater knowledge of the truth. He could have stood as a bridge builder, even rebuking Jewish believers' racism toward their Gentile brothers and sisters. Instead he waffled under the pressure.

Conviction Is Birthed

Peter had been convicted to welcome and accept Gentile believers as full members of God's family, born out his heavenly vision in Acts 10. And with humility, he accepted that conviction. Yet he "backslid" into his former attitude. Seeing Peter's actions and how it was affecting the community, a conviction was birthed with Paul regarding the integrity of the gospel, discipleship, and the inclusion of Gentiles.

Holy Confrontation

"Peter, you are out of step with the gospel." Paul openly confronted and rebuked Peter for hypocritical and partial behavior. Paul stood against Peter's hypocrisy because it was harmful to Peter, to the spiritual development of the Jews and Gentiles, and to the gospel. Paul called Peter out and called him into practicing a whole gospel.

Paul saw a wrong and immediately worked to correct it.

That confrontation leads us back to conviction and reconciliation. Though the text doesn't directly address it, we can hope that

Paul's righteous stance against wrongdoing brought clarity, humility, and repentance back to his brothers in Christ.

CULTURAL SUPERIORITY AND INFERIORITY

Peter's experience is similar to ours in America. Like Peter, the church has had the truth of the gospel. Yet because of humanity's wickedness and the benefits and privileges that these social constructs provide, we have harmed other image bearers, impeding their right to flourish.

While growing up, my (Hazen's) family had membership at one of the most exclusive country clubs in Atlanta. I took tennis lessons there, participated on the club swim team, and celebrated Christmas at the annual banquet. All the membership were White and many were professing Christians, while the vast majority of staff were Black. This never struck me as odd, because that was just my world. I didn't realize at the time that I was growing up receiving an unconscious message that because I was White, I was somehow superior. I never would have said that aloud—nor did I ever hear anybody utter those words about being White. It was just . . . *there*.

I (Josh), on the other hand, grew up in the hood. At least four trap houses (drug dealers) existed on our block. And the sounds that filled our neighborhood weren't children laughing and playing outside, but rather gunfire. Though my family wasn't rich, my mother provided well for my two siblings and me. We never lacked anything we needed.

Throughout my elementary and some of my middle school years, I enjoyed learning and had amazing teachers, most of whom were Black women. But we were limited in our resources, suffering in meager facilities, with dated books, less staff, poor equipment, and overcrowding in the classroom. Because my mother wanted better opportunities for me, when I entered seventh grade, she managed to transfer me to another school—a "better" school.

My new school was immaculate. The halls were expansive. The lunchroom was huge. They had a marching band, a metal shop, and a jazz choir. And most notably, this school had White people. A lot of White people. The students. The teachers. The parents. All White. Except for me.

I had never considered my race or my culture before then. But it was impossible not to in that new school. I had been pulled from the warmth of Black and Brown people and immediately felt the frigid temperature of an all-White environment. Though I couldn't articulate it, I was having a cultural crisis.

From the moment I stepped into the hall the first day, I felt it. Different. I arrived wearing my FUBU jersey, jeans, and some fresh Nike Air Force 1s. Everyone around me was decked out in American Eagle, Aeropostale, Birkenstocks, and Doc Martens.

It was bad enough that I was an awkward seventh grader—highly insecure and self conscious. And add to that, it was clear that I didn't belong.

I had a decision to make. I could either fit in or flame out. I did the former. I began to make friends. Well, let's just say I became everyone's Black friend. I changed the way I spoke, following a more White cadence of speech. I even changed the way I dressed, trading my Iversons for Adidas Superstars. The weekends I used to spend on the basketball court with my cousins quickly became times to hang out at my White friends' expansive homes. I was assimilating.

By changing schools and cultures, I received the message that to be White was to be better or superior. All other groups or cultures were "ghetto" or "hood." And when other students, including my friends and teachers, made some racist comment or called me the N-word or touched and commented on my afro, I received that message loud and clear too—*Hey, Josh, you're Black.*

Soon I began to disdain all things Black. I began to see Black people and culture as less than, as inferior. I began to hate the things that made me, well, me. In every way, I felt inferior. I began to believe that life would be better if I had been born White. And that self-talk eroded my confidence more and more.

There's a real problem with this false and mythical sense of superiority and inferiority, particularly when it seeps into the minds and hearts of Christians, because God never created superior or inferior human beings.

This idea of superiority and inferiority started all the way back at the fall. When sin entered the world, the evil one perverted God's design over our understanding of ourselves and our responsibility on the earth. God created us equal with each other, and together we were to hold dominion over God's created order. But sin twisted that design, so that we began to believe some people were "more equal" than others and that "lesser" humans did not bear the imago Dei. Additionally, we began to believe that dominion was to rule over creation, *including* other human beings.

God never assigned authority to humankind to have dominion over humankind. This is a violation of the created order and does harm to the Creator's creation. And *all* humans bear the imago Dei. Though sin covered, concealed, and committed harm to our understanding of it, in no way did it ever reduce it.

We see this arrogance played out throughout human history. The Egyptians thought themselves superior to the Hebrews and eventually enslaved them. Jews thought of themselves as superior to Gentiles and limited their ability to worship God in the temple. And in the United States, the force of majority culture believed White people superior to all others and thus should possess dominance over them.

If we are not careful, we can unconsciously absorb and internalize much of the toxicity that is present in our racialized society and cultural messages. We can even begin to engage the world through the warped lens of superiority or inferiority. And soon it manifests itself through the supremacy of one group, hatred of others and/or self, social caste systems, colorism, and pride resulting in an inferiority and superiority complex held by all. For those of us in America, this superiority/inferiority myth represents both the trauma of being a POC and the trauma of being White. And our sinful arrogance perpetrates the myth.

"Myths are powerful because they are believed and therefore become the basis of our actions as individuals, as families, and as a society as a whole," explains Dr. Tony Evans. "Myths develop like a pearl inside an oyster's shell. When a grain of sand gets caught in the oyster's shell, it is continually coated by the secretions of the oyster until a valuable pearl is formed. In the same way the continuous secretions of societal standards, justified religious principles, create a mythical pearl that is accepted as both valid and valuable by society."[5] This illustrates how we arrive at some of the racial conclusions and ideas we espouse. Only by understanding their roots and identifying the lies can we embrace cultural humility and own our stories.

Throughout American history to be White was synonymous with being part of the ruling class. To be White was to possess power, which afforded one privilege and social capital. Whereas the inverse was true for people of color, in which a Black or Brown person was relegated to a second-class citizenship.

> If we, like Paul, were to affirm the God-given dignity of the other, the church would emerge as a beacon of hope and light among the nations.

Consider the four-hundred-year narrative. The idea of *Black* became prominent with the transatlantic slave trade in which race became used as a caste system to distinguish enslaved people from the ruling class. *White* then became synonymous with power and supremacy. With each person dehumanized through slavery and then Jim Crow, the myth of superiority and inferiority reinforced itself, strengthening the notion of who belongs and who does not, who is worthy and who isn't. This story is hundreds of years in the making.

Rasool Berry, teaching pastor at The Bridge Church in Brooklyn, New York, astutely observed,

> Christians should be aware of how our sin often blinds us and makes us susceptible to using culture and power for self-justification. Culture often blinds us to what the Bible is saying. Power allows us to insist that our blinded version of reality MUST BE TRUE. Look at Peter—an apostle!— he let his Jewish upbringing keep him from eating with his fellow Gentile believers (Galatians 2:11–13). His culture blinded him to his wrong-doing, and his power as an apostle permitted the status quo that kept the Gentiles as second-class citizens in the church; that was, until Paul used his power as an apostle to publicly critique Peter's abuse of power (Galatians 2:14).[6]

Culture and power can blind us to the truth of the gospel and God's created order. This is what we witnessed with Peter and Paul. Culture and power took over Peter, causing him to participate in the sin of cultural superiority. It is much the same for us.

If we, like Paul, were to affirm the God-given dignity of the other, the church would emerge as a beacon of hope and light among the nations. But too often we have not. As Tony Evans observed, "Acceptance of the myth that African Americans are inferior to Anglos has had catastrophic consequences for the psyche of black people, the worldview of white people, and harmony among the races. Worst of all, it has hindered the church from being salt and light in America."[7]

The over emphasis of the imago Dei in our White brothers and sisters is traumatic to the White soul and catastrophically impacts the Black and Brown soul. We were never meant to have dominion over people, nor to exist in a caste system. We must never forget that behind race exists actual image bearers of God. The enduring harm that has been committed must never be underestimated and it must be owned if we as the family of God are able to move forward.

THE PATH TO CULTURAL HUMILITY

White people have a culture—their own "customary beliefs, social forms, material traits . . . shared attitudes, values, goals, and practices."[8] Black and Brown people have a culture too. Each culture is informed by upbringing, traditions of our ethnic heritage, the environment we are raised in, the values we choose to live by, the laws and history of our country. In fact, within the United States, we have many cultures housed in one dominant culture—meaning subsets within culture that allow for difference and a synchronization of other cultures. Dr. Soong-Chan Rah expands the definition of culture by explaining that "it is a human attempt to understand the world around us. It is the programming that shapes who we are and who we are becoming. It is a social system that is shaped by the individual and that also has the capacity to shape the individual. But it is also the presence of God, the image of God, the mission of God found in the human spirit, soul, and social system."[9]

Difference is good and okay. It becomes a weapon of mass destruction when we seek to impose our values, beliefs, and practices on those around us, believing that ours are superior—which sends the message that *we* are superior. As Dr. John Perkins once told us, "There is no reconciliation until you recognize the dignity of the other." And to do that requires humility. So let's consider some ways to own our stories by pursuing cultural humility.

Affirm the Truth and Reject the Lie

It was a process for me (Josh) to embrace that I was a Black man specifically created that way by a God who lavishes His love on me (see 1 John 3:1). I had to affirm the truth of the imago Dei within me and reject the lie that told me that by being Black, I was somehow inferior. For all the anti-Black messages—both intentional and unintentional—I ingested daily, for all of the toxic effects of White culture on me, for the impact of the social constructs of the present, I had to affirm the truth about who I am.

> This humility means that we right size the imago Dei in all people. No one is superior, no one is inferior, all are created to reflect the beauty of God.

For people of color, self love is the beginning of rejecting the lie of inferiority. We are loved and created to reflect the beauty and wonder of God. Black and Brown people are made in the image of God. There is no inferiority in that image. There is no secondary, minor, nor subordination in that image. He is God, and we reflect Him. This gives us value, worth, and dignity. We must affirm and inform our God-given dignity.

White people too are created in the image and likeness of God. This means there is inherent beauty and worth in them as well. God impressed His image upon the White soul and White people stand as a testimony to the goodness and beauty of God.

This appreciation and understanding of one another and how

distinctions are equally loved and created by God builds within us a humility to recognize our culture isn't superior or inferior, just as we aren't superior or inferior. That kind of humility allows us to embrace our own culture and others' culture and allow God to be praised and honored through both.

This humility means that we right size the imago Dei in all people. No one is superior, no one is inferior, all are created to reflect the beauty of God. Our bias is of the fallen nature and must be crucified, sanctified, and conformed to the image of Christ.

As fallen people, we are corrupt and broken in ways that we can't fathom and understand. We each must be honest about how, in many instances, majority culture has shaped us all to see people of color as secondary citizens. Accepting this truth is the on-ramp to authentic engagement with the work of reconciliation.

We play our part in owning the story by recognizing our own patterns of thought and action, and then bringing the carnal thoughts and attitudes into obedience to Christ. We understand this issue with any other sin pattern, such as pride, anger, lust, or laziness. However, when we try to address the clusters of sinful attitudes, we harbor regarding superior or inferior people, many of us prefer to deny our need to have our minds renewed (see Eph. 4:23). We must recognize that we need to address these patterns in the battlefields of our minds.

Howard Thurman, a notable mentor to Dr. King, once said, "If a man is convinced that he is safe only as long as he uses his power to give others a sense of insecurity, then the measure of their security is in his hands. If security or insecurity is at the mercy of a single individual or group, then control of behavior becomes routine."[10] What we witness by cultural norms and power dynamics in the workplace, church, and American society supports the notion of inferiority and superiority. We must be active in repudiating such ideas.

On a recent phone call with Dr. Perkins, he stated: "You don't give people dignity, you affirm it." That's where we as people must go.

Serve One Another in Love—Go Even Lower

I (Josh) loathe the word *humility*. Everything in my flesh cringes at the sound of it, because I know it requires me to lay down my rights and my pride with the promise of receiving nothing in return, except the joy of suffering for the Savior. That's ultimately what servanthood is about. Sacrifice.

Jesus told us what God-honoring service is supposed to look like. During Jesus' time on earth, Israel was under Roman rule. In Roman culture, as soldiers passed through a town, they could randomly pick a local person and require him to serve them by traveling a mile's distance with them. This act of service consisted of shouldering their ruck, which contained weaponry, food, clothing, and any essential personal items. It was certainly heavy. And to be clear, this wasn't a voluntary role. The locals had no say in the matter, nor could they refuse. So when Jesus told His listeners, "If anyone forces you to go one mile, go with him two miles" (Matt. 5:41), this would have been disconcerting, even absurd. But this is the way of the kingdom—that in humility, we offer ourselves and our rights to others so we honor God. When our "enemy" tells us to "go low," we respond by going even lower. As humiliating as this dynamic must have been, Jesus was essentially saying, "Serve one another in love, even in situations that may not be the most favorable of circumstances."

We too must take that posture. We are commanded to live counter-culturally, to forge a path in the upside-down kingdom.

The path to cultural humility is paved with, well, humility. There is no understating its cost, because it will cost us everything, and will still require us to go lower for the sake of the gospel.

Do the Heart Work

Bishop Claude Alexander once stated, "It may not be your fault, but it is your problem." The racial situation in America may not be our fault, but as believers we do have a responsibility to humbly do the heart work in order to own the story.

As a White reconciler, I (Hazen) recognize I need to persevere through to keep my heart healthy and engaged, because the temptation can lead me toward denial, guilt, and fatigue.

Denial comes in our unwillingness to recognize there is a genuine place within each of us in need of change. No one has freed themselves fully from the sins of partiality, pride, anger, mistrust, or selfishness that compose the stronghold of racism. I know I battle these in different forms every day. Just because I may enjoy a measure of freedom from these ungodly attitudes doesn't equal holiness. There is always more righteousness to grow in!

Jesus rebuked the Laodicean church in Revelation because they thought they had "arrived": "You say, 'I am rich; I have acquired wealth and *do not need a thing.*' But you do not realize that you are wretched, pitiful, poor, blind and naked" (Rev. 3:17 NIV). Wherever we think we have no need for change and have arrived, we are in denial and are ripe for God's invitation into a deeper humility. We don't want to deny our need for God in any area, but instead embrace it with a healthy poverty of spirit.

The heart sickness of guilt comes when we stop denying our sinful tendencies around race and acknowledge them—but neglect to take them to the right place, the cross. We might be tempted to try to fix our issues on your own, but this is where gospel-centered reconciliation differs from what the world offers. We cannot fix ourselves or the world around us on our own; it is only the power of God's grace by the Holy Spirit that can change us as we walk with Him. Even in the midst of our imperfection and brokenness, trying to do right but failing, we can still be confident that we are loved and accepted by God.

As a White man, though I may struggle with racial sins that are condemnable, Christ's death on the cross was where He condemned that sin and paid for it, so I can go there and be forgiven, set free, and changed. Guilt won't heal our racism issue but acknowledgment, repentance, and receipt of His forgiveness will!

Lastly, there is the heart sickness of fatigue. We may work so hard to try to do right by our brothers and sisters of color but still fail and say the wrong thing, do the wrong thing, or neglect to do the right thing, and then we have to get back up and try again. Progress in transformation is slow and the going can be tough. This is the hard and narrow road of being a disciple of Jesus Christ.

As reconcilers we strive for righteousness and justice in our lives, families, and the world around us, and yet it remains at times two steps forward, one step back. The story of the gospel is a love story, but the context of the story in this life is a war zone. Take heart, reconciler, we can have confidence in the midst of the suffering that the ultimate redemption we long for will come with God's kingdom. Furthermore, we have the promises of God to hold fast to. If we persevere in doing what is right, we will bear fruit! Remember Paul's words, "Let us not grow weary of doing good, for in due season we will reap, if we do not give up" (Gal. 6:9).

For me (Josh), as a person of color, the difficult heart work is often where I fall short in my pursuit of cultural humility. As tough as it is to admit as a Christian, I have had periods in which I greatly resented my White siblings. In an effort to self preserve because of racial trauma, at times I have retreated, lashed out, and deeply wounded. Those were times that certainly did not honor Christ. I struggle too with fatigue and frustration, because I often sense that I am continually signing up for cultural humility by coming to the bridge of reconciliation and yielding parts of myself to engage with the broad part of culture. I know many people of color struggle with this fatigue as well. We do this each and every day because most spaces are White dominant. I had a dear friend, Anna, suffering from reconciliation fatigue, who told me:

> We exist in their world. American culture is created by the majority, so they are the powerful. Minorities are immediately disadvantaged by mere numbers. Then if we add racial history and intentional oppression of minority groups to the equation, well, we have our present plight.
>
> Think of it this way, 90 percent of all people are right-hand dominant. Left-hand dominant people comprise only 10 percent of the world's population. Imagine intentionally opposing, undermining, and oppressing left-handed people [which actually did happen, by the way, particularly in schools]. This is the very situation the Black community finds itself in.

On both sides, owning the story by doing the necessary heart work is essential. For people of color, we must gird ourselves not to grow fatigue in reconciliation work—especially when we become disappointed with our brothers and sisters of the majority because of their lack of effort to see us and our continued vulnerability. We stand on the bridge continually willing to engage on mostly the majority's terms. It takes heart work not to grow weary.

For White reconcilers, we must also do the heart work that keeps us from looking away and retreating. We must own that we may not know much about the Black or Brown experience and how they have had to assimilate, and at times felt the pull to give up who they were created to be in order to "fit in."

We are all called to be part of a family, a body, the bride of

Christ. We must humbly practice forgiveness and set healthy, godly boundaries. For the body of Christ to become whole and holy, we must pursue sanctification together. It is the only path forward. We must pursue holiness, and righteousness in our living, seeking to represent Christ in a world that needs to see Him. We must sacrificially and humbly love one another deeply, so much so that we are willing to go low and participate in healing and reconciling the body of Christ.

If one of the original apostles, Peter, found himself struggling with racism and insecurity, we must not mistakenly believe we are exempt from the temptation. We have a choice: we can follow Peter's example or Paul's. May we, by God's grace and the Holy Spirit's leading, continually choose Paul's.

9

Change the Story

Around the four hundredth year of Egyptian enslavement, the Lord raised up a deliverer for the Israelites: Moses. A reluctant leader, marred with imperfection, Moses spoke prophetically to the powers of the day and the system of oppression and injustice, declaring this as the moment for liberation, the moment for salvation. And God used him to free the children of Israel.

After around four hundred years of silence between testaments, the Lord raised up the ultimate deliverer: Jesus Christ, the Righteous. The One on whose shoulders a new government was borne. Jesus, the progenitor of salvation. The One who brought reconciliation between God and man and made provision for brother and sister to be reconciled into one new humanity. The One who came and set the captives free, liberating the beloved "whosoever."

We find ourselves at another inflection point. In 2019, we commemorated the four hundredth year since enslaved people were introduced into the colonies, which later became the United States of America. And the Lord is raising up a new kind of deliverer: the church. The church, who standing on the gospel, will boldly declare the truth therein—that God has created all people in His image and in His likeness. The church, who will use her governmental authority as the ekklesia (the witnessing body) to proclaim that God, through His Son, Jesus, has provided a means for us to be reconciled to Him and to each other. For it is indeed the Father's desire for us to be one, a diverse beautiful family.

We are the deliverers God is using to change the story of where we are headed. Our collective past does not have to dictate our collective future. Redemption allows us to write a different story, one that testifies of the goodness of Jesus and His people boldly pursuing righteousness, mercy, and justice, forging a path toward reconciliation.

> Mercy, righteousness, and justice are caught in an unquenchable love affair that has been burning since the beginning of time.

If we are going to emerge as what Dr. King called the prophetic "conscience of the state,"[1] we must commit to pursuing a few things through compassionate action and sacrificial love: (1) reckoning—that we identify and call out our poor doctrinal positions that have held the evangelical church captive for centuries; (2) repenting—that our heads, hearts, and hands must come into alignment and that we continually seek the fruit of our change; (3) repairing—that we call the church to mend the damage of communities and people groups that have been historically harmed, and that we move forward armed with the truth of the gospel, which rightly esteems the work of righteousness, mercy, and justice, so we can mend.

We live in a world steeped in false binaries. To be about morality is to be against compassion, or to be about gospel-centered compassion, one must be loose on morality. This is also true of the church regarding righteousness, mercy, and justice. Some will proclaim that the church should just preach salvation, referring to a narrow aspect of the gospel that ignores the social action of Micah 6:8—to "do justice, and to love kindness, and to walk humbly with your God"—while others emphasize only justice and action, disregarding the righteous standard we've been called to through the gospel. We must reject the lie that our responsibility is an *either/or* and that we have to choose only one. The Good News of Jesus Christ is *both/and*. We must pursue a marriage of both to truly capture the heart of God. The idea that we must choose sides is steeped in fallacy. The peculiarity of the believer should be apparent in that we love like no other by enacting these both/and principles in our families, communities, and nation.

We should seek to live as salt and light in a world that desperately needs to taste and see it. There isn't a conflict between these two "sides," as there is no conflict in the heart of the Lord. Mercy, righteousness, and justice are caught in an unquenchable love affair that has been burning since the beginning of time. In fact, God is so serious about these virtues that the psalmist depict God's throne as being founded upon them: "Righteousness and justice are the foundation of your throne; steadfast love [mercy] and faithfulness go before you" (Ps. 89:14). At the heart of changing the story is cultivating a heart of mercy, and out of that merciful heart flows righteousness and justice. The three are inextricably bound.

As Dr. King said, "If the church will free itself from the shackles of a deadening status quo, and, recovering its great historic mission, will proceed to speak and act fearlessly and insistently on the questions of justice and peace, it will enkindle the imagination of mankind. It will fire the souls of men and imbue them with a glowing and ardent love for truth, justice, and peace. Men far and near will then see the church as that great fellowship of love which provides light and bread for lonely travellers at midnight."[2]

It's time to change the story.

CHANGE THROUGH RECKONING

The summer of 2020 saw protests and demonstrations break out across the nation in reaction to the racial unrest and violence of several key murders of Black people. Ahmaud Arbery was a young man gunned down by two White civilians on February 23 as he was jogging near his home in Glynn County, Georgia. Breonna Taylor was a young lady shot and killed by police at her home in Louisville, Kentucky, when officers mistakenly served a no-knock warrant to her residence shortly after midnight. Suspected of a crime, Minneapolis resident George Floyd was physically restrained by an officer on May 25, who placed a knee on Floyd's neck for more than nine minutes, suffocating him, which led to Floyd's death. And Rayshard Brooks, an African American shot and killed by police on June 12 outside an Atlanta Wendy's restaurant.

> A gospel that fails to call believers to righteousness, mercy, and justice lacks the very substance that composes our salvation.

Though all of them were horrific, the Brooks shooting lay especially hard on our hearts, because that was in our town. We knew that while the protests and marches were taking place, we needed the church to be represented. We wanted to grieve, lament, and intercede on behalf of our city and nation. So we reached out to leaders and church members through-out Atlanta and asked them to gather together each Sunday at the site of the protests for as long as they continued. A few hundred of us showed up and began praying and calling on God to intercede and bring reconciliation. On one of those Sundays, a lady wan-dered up to hear what we were doing. After observing for several minutes, she shouted, "Where has the church been in all this? No, no, no! No more worship. No more preaching. No more church. It's time for the church to *be* the church. It's time for action."

Her words were indicting. Her words were convicting. Her words were true.

To journey toward a reconciled church, we must reckon with the truth about the church's hole in the gospel and their inaction in matters that break the heart of God. Any gospel narrative that does not center on the Person and actions of Jesus or doesn't prioritize compassionate action for neighbor is anemic. A gos-pel that fails to call believers to righteousness, mercy, and justice lacks the very substance that composes our salvation. It's time for the church to start living out compassionate action.

In reckoning, each of us must take the knowledge and owner-ship we've acquired and committed to and apply that to correcting our approach. God takes no pleasure in the perversion of truth. So we intentionally shed our broken and misguided understanding of image Dei within every person and grapple with the Scriptures and doctrinal positions in fresh and new ways. We acknowledge the ways in which the church has perverted the concepts of righteous-ness, mercy, and justice. Reckoning includes being vigilant about ways in which the church continues to fall short, to confront those places, and work to ensure that we change.

Part of reckoning with compassionate action is that our White brothers and sisters call out the evil that has been perpetrated against people of color. Part of reckoning with compassionate action also calls on Christians of color to be merciful toward our White siblings, righteous in our dealings, and to hold the line concerning justice.

Reckoning is the first step in changing the story. And though all of reconciliation work is difficult, that first step is always the toughest. It means we move from head and heart to hands and feet—requiring the most humility. It's hard to show up to a fight wholehearted when racial injustice and debates continue in our culture and in the church. And yet we follow in the footsteps of Jesus, the Great Reconciler, who paves our way and gives us the strength to keep reconciling. We must trust that even out of our imperfect work, He can give beauty for ashes and joy for our sorrow.

Reckoning calls us to come to see that our faith has been informed by culture far more than by Christ regarding issues of human dignity and equality. Where notions of supremacy and nationalism have seasoned our gospel, the church becomes powerless. Finally, if in our pursuit of righteousness we are not compelled to make wrong things right by enacting justice on behalf of our Black and Brown siblings, we exclaim in the loudest possible terms, *I am a prisoner of America and not of Christ.*

We all must do our part in reckoning with a broken theology and our broken past. It's a journey we should take together, because when pursued together, we can experience the sweet power of unity and healing that God deserves for us.

CHANGE THROUGH REPENTANCE'S FRUIT

Not long ago, Hazen and I were with a White man that made some less-than-savory comments about the Black community as a whole. I often hesitate to reply to such statements, since I know how Black people can be framed as aggressive or angry when we respond directly to ignorance, so usually I'll just redirect so as not to dignify such comments. On this particular occasion, I was set to let it pass without confronting it, but feeling frustrated that once again a Christian spoke without knowledge or compassion.

But Hazen piped up and offered this person a full education and rebuke for his comment. Though he did so in love, he was firm enough to let this person know he had crossed a line. And an amazing thing happened: Hazen's action so convicted our White sibling that he repented. Today this person is making strides concerning race.

Though we discussed repentance in the previous chapters on ownership, it also falls into the change part. One way we see how repentance changes the story is by the fruit—something we must consistently look for.

Let's take our cue from the shepherd-turned-prophet, Amos. The Lord used Amos mightily to pronounce judgment against Israel, who had become a synchronistic people, combining the worship of other gods alongside the worship of Yahweh. Additionally, they were grossly indulging in sexual immorality, idolatry, and greed, as well as exploiting the poor and selling their brothers into slavery for financial expediency. Sound familiar? We can see

> God desires justice *from* all people and *for* all people.

much of the history and tragedy of America entwined with the actions of this nation. After the Lord identifies their sin, he talks through his prophet about the fruit of their repentance:

> I hate, I despise your feasts, and I take no delight in your solemn assemblies. Even though you offer me your burnt

offerings and grain offerings, I will not accept them; and the peace offerings of your fattened animals, I will not look upon them. Take away from me the noise of your songs; to the melody of your harps I will not listen. But let justice roll down like waters, and righteousness like an ever-flowing stream. (Amos 5:21–24)

We can sum up this passage in Amos in this simple statement: fruit-bearing always follows repentance. If there is no fruit, then there hasn't been authentic repentance. Though Israel was practicing the religious trappings of their faith, they were disconnected from a heart bent on serving God and loving neighbor. So God, in very strong terms, made clear what He thought about their actions: they were worthless!

He started by informing the nation of His desires by first telling them what He did not want. Then he moved to say what was lacking: righteousness and justice. God desires a heart bent toward merciful action manifesting in righteous and just ways on behalf of people who are created and shaped in the image of God. In other words, God desires justice *from* all people and *for* all people. The ability to pursue and receive justice comes as a result (or fruit) of repentance.

Let's hone in on justice as it relates to repentance. Repentance is best defined by two steps: (1) Contrition over our sin. We rightly acknowledge that we have traded God's way for our way. (2) Bearing fruit that reflects a change of heart. We begin to practice opposite behavior. Often in reconciliation work people place a greater emphasis on contrition related to repentance. This is right, as we should be broken over our sin. Yet we *also* should be committed to bearing fruit in keeping with repentance, as this is the proof that real transformation (change) has taken place. As

Jesus commanded, "Produce fruit in keeping with repentance" (Luke 3:8 niv).

What does this look for the believer? Works of justice.

As Dr. John Perkins says, "Justice is any act of reconciliation that restores any part of God's creation back to its original intent, purpose, or image. When I think about justice that way, it doesn't surprise me at all that God loves it. It includes both the acts of social justice and the restorative justice found on the cross."[3]

> We cannot become (or remain) moderates. It is not enough to silently agree.

When we work toward justice, we are joining the work of God by co-laboring toward the desire of His heart: reconciliation. In Colossians, Paul clearly stated Christ's intentions: "In him all the fullness of God was pleased to dwell, and through him to reconcile to himself all things, whether on earth or in heaven, making peace by the blood of his cross" (1:19–20).

In pursuit of justice, we are joining the work of God. We are partnering with the King of the universe to support the idea of His kingdom coming on earth as it is in heaven. We are moving toward the ultimate goal: reconciliation between the Creator and His creation.

We, like Amos, must become proclaimers of the Lord's heart for justice. We cannot become (or remain) moderates. It is not enough to silently agree. As Dr. Martin Luther King, Jr. wrote, "He who passively accepts evil is as much involved in it as he who helps to perpetrate it. He who accepts evil without protesting against it is really cooperating with it."[4] We must be vocal proponents for justice, which is synonymous with changing the story.

We must practice justice. In our various spheres of influence, there is so much good and change we can affect. No one is rendered helpless in the fight for racial unity. No one. We must leverage our positions for the good of unity and to bring dignity to all who possess imago Dei. Perhaps you lead a church. You can create an environment in which all nations and people are welcomed and included. This doesn't mean you race out and find a token representation. It means that you include people across cultures, races, ethnicities, and genders to be vital parts of informing the direction and expression of the local congregation. Eleven o'clock will continue to be segregated, unless we take proactive steps to correct the underlying problems. This, too, is justice.

The Lord didn't tell the people through Amos that He wanted justice to trickle through their society. The New Living Translation uses the phrase *mighty flood of justice* to describe what God wanted to see (Amos 5:24). As Dr. John Perkins explained, "Justice is a process, and change takes time, but I believe we ought to dream big dreams and make big statements as we pursue those dreams."[5] We must desire the same.

CHANGE THROUGH REPAIRING

If we are going to emerge as credible in our witness to the world, we must champion repairing that which has been damaged, lost, or stolen, because of racism. We must pursue a higher ethic, which is love. We must correct our orthodoxy, what we believe. We must correct our orthopathy, what we feel. We must correct our orthopraxy, how we practice both. The fruit of our righteousness and justice working together should look and feel like love to the world. We can do it. We can emerge as the credible witness Christ so desires by the change of repairing. Let's take our cue from a wee little man, Zacchaeus.

Zacchaeus was a wealthy tax collector. He was curious about Jesus; certainly he had heard the stories. Because he was a short man, he couldn't see Jesus through the crowds as He was passing by. So Zacchaeus had to do extreme things to gain an audience with Jesus—he climbed a tree. That got Jesus' attention, who then invited Himself to Zacchaeus's home. Zacchaeus, moved to repentance, bore the fruit of justice right away:

> Zacchaeus stood up and said to the Lord, "Look, Lord! Here and now I give half of my possessions to the poor, and if I have cheated anybody out of anything, I will pay back four times the amount."
>
> Jesus said to him, "Today salvation has come to this house, because this man, too, is a son of Abraham." (Luke 19:8–9 NIV)

Zacchaeus willingly took his ill-gotten profits and acted mercifully and justly to repair and change the story. This was fruit, proof, of his transformed heart. Am I suggesting a salvation-by-works sort of gospel? No, actually the inverse: when we are saved, our hearts are transformed, and through sanctification, being formed into the image of Christ by the power of the Holy Spirit, we begin to pursue actions in keeping with that transformation. We must note that Zacchaeus wasn't saved because of his actions; his actions demonstrated his salvation or the authenticity of his repentance. And he followed the biblical model, according to the law, for making restitution (see Ex. 22:12–36; Num. 5:7; Prov. 14:9). It was then that Jesus pronounced, "Today salvation has come to this house, because this man, too, is a son of Abraham."

It was the fruit of a repentant heart that demonstrated that he had been transformed by the power of God and that he was willing to act to repair the story.

There is a lot of conjecture around reparations and restitution. Though we don't have enough space and time to do a service to the contention, we can see from this passage and others like it that repair is a part of the way of the kingdom. We witness it in the story of Zacchaeus, and ultimately the whole narrative of the gospel is about repairing the breach that sin wrought.

WHAT CHANGE LOOKS LIKE IN PRACTICE

How do we begin in changing the story? In making repair, what am I calling the church to do? How can we be part of the solution, considering all that has happened racially over the past four centuries? We must follow the example of Zacchaeus and the example of Christ. Paul shows us what following Jesus' example includes:

> Let each of you look not only to his own interests, but also to the interests of others. Have this mind among yourselves, which is yours in Christ Jesus, who, though he was in the form of God, did not count equality with God a thing to be grasped, but emptied himself, by taking the form of a servant, being born in the likeness of men. And being found in human form, he humbled himself by becoming obedient to the point of death, even death on a cross. (Phil. 2:4–8)

Through Christ's example in the condescension, He demonstrated how we must leverage what we have for just outcomes in the best interest of others. Like Jesus, we must place the interests of others above our own. Like Jesus, we must humble ourselves and shoulder our cross. As we do so, we are able to leverage our power, position, and privilege for the sake of justice and reconciliation. Let's look a bit at each of those leverages.

Leverage Our Power

Jesus held all power in His hands. Yet he didn't count that as a thing to be grasped. Instead Jesus leveraged His power through His humility and obedience to the cross. We too must consider the ways in which we can leverage the power we have in this life to attain the best interest of others. The OneRace board are some of the most gifted and influential people in Atlanta. Each one leverages his or her power and expertise as attorneys, pastors, community leaders, and business people for the work of reconciliation. Black, White, Hispanic, Asian; male and female—they all use their power to advance the mission of OneRace, enabling us to impact thousands of lives with the gospel.

We can ask ourselves: In what ways can I leverage the power I possess—my time, talent, and finances—to secure just outcomes for others?

If you aren't sure, ask God to show you. Then leverage that in your pursuit of becoming a reconciler.

Leverage Our Position

Jesus is 100 percent God and 100 percent human. In the condescension, Jesus put on flesh to walk among and ultimately redeem humanity. He leveraged His position as God by coming as a holy and righteous sacrifice on our behalf. He leveraged His position as human in that He was tempted by sin in all the ways that women and men are, yet He never succumbed to them. He is the sinless Lamb of God.

Josh and Susan Robinson have leveraged their positions as White professionals to pursue justice for others. Susan is the co-host of a podcast called Race and Redemption, engaging White Christians in the work of reconciliation and bridge building. Josh is the chairman of a school committed to offering premiere education to Black and Brown students in English Avenue, a neighborhood in West Atlanta that is fraught with poverty and a poor education system. They're quite literally leveraging their position as influential individuals with access to wealthy circles in order to repair and affect change within Black and Brown communities.

We too are invited to leverage our positions. We must ask ourselves: In what ways can I follow the example of Jesus and leverage my position or station in life as a _____ (parent, pastor, friend, professor) to bring about more just outcomes? How can I leverage all that I have amassed to repair the damage that racism has committed to my brothers and sisters and to society as a whole?

Leverage Our Privilege

Being God's Son, being part of the Godhead, possessing all power, certainly Jesus had privilege when He came to earth as a man. He never reduced His status as God, but He emptied Himself—meaning, in the condescension, He submitted Himself, according to His own will and the desire of the Father to the work of the cross. Jesus leveraged His privilege to secure salvation on our behalf.

LaTonya Gates is a justice advocate in her work as founder and executive director of PAWKids, an organization to empower and encourage self-sufficiency and to cultivate life and hope through radical service. In 2014, she listened to her pastor preach on the importance of taking church beyond the four walls of their building. The message sparked a vision within her:

> I couldn't understand how we on the Westside share the 30318 ZIP code with Buckhead [a wealthy community], yet we have homes with no water, so much homelessness, squatters, the second lowest ranking school in the

state—much different than when you cross the tracks into Buckhead. I had an idea to bring people together from different socioeconomic backgrounds to bridge the gap, then empower my neighborhood by leading resources where they don't exist.[6]

That idea soon became PAWKids. She took action by starting an organization that feeds, mentors, and educates the next generation of Black and Brown young people of her community. Hundreds of young people and families have been impacted by her work. She is fighting for justice and her corner of the city is just a bit brighter because of her gospel witness.

"We all have privilege," she said. "As a Black woman, mine is to go to my community and provide the resources they need to survive and thrive."[7]

Susan Robinson, who co-hosts the Race and Redemption podcast, is leveraging her privilege as a White woman to speak to other White people about race and to call them to be reconcilers.

We too must ask ourselves: In what ways am I privileged? For our White siblings, it may be that you have the ability to speak into the lives of other Whites to open their minds and hearts to the reality of racism in the church and in the world and to encourage them to become reconcilers. For our siblings of color, it may be, like LaTonya, to consider the ways we can advocate and provide the resources our siblings and communities need to repair and change their stories.

A CHARGE TO THE CHURCH

As in the story of the Good Samaritan, the church must get involved in repairing and healing the wrongs that have been committed against people of color and we must commit to reversing the curse of racism. The church has a great opportunity to emerge as a proponent of repairing the chasm that racism has wrought. Mercy, righteousness, and justice is the only path forward.

Thank goodness the Good Samaritan didn't look upon the bloody, beaten, half-dead man and say, "I didn't do this" or "This is not my fault." Rather, the man was struck with tremendous conviction, "If I don't act, who will?" Then he moved with compassion and engaged with a problem for which society as a whole was culpable. Let's never forget the reputation of that Jericho road; it was notorious for crime. Yet this social outcast acted mercifully and enacted justice on the man's behalf. We must go and do the same.

We are called to see ourselves as a collective and to get involved in the affairs that affect our Black and Brown siblings. Dr. King spelled out this charge as he reflected over the Jericho road situation:

> On the one hand we are called to play the good Samaritan on life's roadside; but that will be only an initial act. One day we must come to see that the whole Jericho road must be transformed so that men and women will not be constantly beaten and robbed as they make their journey on life's highway. True compassion is more than flinging a coin to a beggar; it is not haphazard and superficial. It comes to see that an edifice which produces beggars needs restructuring.[8]

Together, we can change the story. Together, we can raise the prophetic consciousness of the church back to the Father's standards. But we must all do our part. Change is never easy, nor is it something we should ever pursue lightly. The road is long and the fight is great. There are many injustices that continue to plague society, and our reconciling work can seem like an insurmountable struggle. But as we move forward in our change work, we can carry the words of the apostle Paul with us from 2 Corinthians

4:17–18 (NIV): "Our light and momentary troubles are achieving for us an eternal glory that far outweighs them all. So we fix our eyes not on what is seen, but on what is unseen, since what is seen is temporary, but what is unseen is eternal."

10

Ten Commitments of a Reconciler

A dear friend and mentor, Dr. Crawford Loritts, recently said to me (Josh), "If we are going to be strong, we must get used to lifting heavy things." This is true of reconciliation work. Many people want progress without pain, glory without grind, and a win without work. If we are going to make a positive impact, however, we must be willing to lift heavy things. We must get used to engaging with heavy topics, ideas, and difficult practices. We can take our cue on just how to do that from the prophet Micah.

Israel was wayward and wanted an open relationship with God. They didn't know if they wanted to serve Yahweh or if they wanted to pursue their own passions. Often they attempted to do both as they worshiped other gods and pursued greed, power, sex, and oppression. The prophet Micah confronted the people and gave a clear directive from God, that if Israel wanted to remain in relationship with Yahweh and avoid captivity: "He has told you, O man, what is good; and what does the Lord require of you but to do justice, and to love kindness [mercy], and to walk humbly with your God?" (Mic. 6:8).

That directive hasn't changed. For us to be reconcilers that please God and change the story for the good of the kingdom and this world, we too are called to do justice, love mercy, and walk humbly with God.

The saying goes that we must "make the decision before we need to make the decision." This is principled living. Racial righteousness and racial justice emerge from the soil of principled living. We make commitments about the kind of person we want to be and the kind of world we want to see, so we can orient our lives to make the desired impact. We have a set of values and principles to live by so our lives yield kingdom fruit. As we engage with the heavy lifting of changing the story for generations to come, we do so using the framework Micah offered. And with that framework in place, we offer ten commitments reconcilers can make to see real change take place.

AS WE DO JUSTICE . . .

Commitment 1: Speak Up and Lead Out

Many people strike out into reconciliation work—until it costs them something. Then self-preservation kicks in, and they abandon their pursuit of reconciliation. But as we've mentioned throughout the book, reconciliation will cost us much more than we even know, likely more than we want to sacrifice. Speaking from personal experience, Hazen and I have given more, sacrificed more, and been in more unforgettable conversations than we ever dreamt of. But the fruit has made the difficulty worth it.

As scary and difficult as it is, when faced with heavy racial issues, speak up. Challenge the mindsets of those around you. Challenge systems that oppress. Challenge those in your sphere of influence. Racism isn't just a people of color issue; this must be a humanity issue, a body of Christ issue, *your* issue.

Several years ago, as I (Josh) was taking my son to school, Tom pulled up behind me at a stoplight with his Confederate flag mounted on the back of his vehicle. I will never forget the angst, the rage, or the pain that filled my soul. The thing that really gets me about this scenario is that I wasn't the only one who saw it. But I *was* the only person who spoke up. I embraced the conflict, creating an opportunity for dialogue at the expense of my comfort. I confronted Tom in love and boldness. My statement to him was merely to recap the history of such a symbol and the pain associated with it. But I didn't stop there. I went on to tell him how seeing when someone glorifies a symbol that embodies the oppression and suffering of millions of image bearers of color was a massive challenge for me, my children, and the people of color around him. My decision to be vulnerable and to embrace confrontation brought about change in Tom and change in the environment.

Shortly after Tom took the flag off his vehicle, one of the teachers pulled me aside and thanked me. "As a person of color, it has always offended me," she said. "I simply need this job and couldn't afford to lose it."

I wonder how many people are in situations like hers. I wonder how many people are powerless in the fight for the change they desperately need. When we speak up and lead out we create an opportunity for us and others to experience a two-fold liberation.

First, we liberate those who may be powerless or affected by the post, flag, comment, or action. We use our power for those who need their voices and power amplified in these situations. We must be willing to liberate others and ourselves. In his *Letter from a Birmingham Jail*, Dr. King wrote, "We know through painful experience that freedom is never voluntarily given by the oppressor; it must be demanded by the oppressed."[1] We align ourselves with the oppressed by speaking up and leading out. We demand our liberation and the liberation of our neighbors. We must be willing to take a risk to see freedom come to those around us.

Second, when we speak up and lead out, we create an opportunity for offenders to be liberated as well. Tom, as it turned out, was a great guy. Was he racially ignorant? Yes. But Tom was also a grandfather, son, uncle, husband, brother, US Marine Corps veteran, and fellow believer in Christ. After Tom and I sat together for about an hour, with tears in his eyes, he confessed to being racially ignorant. That's huge. He voiced his desire to know more and to understand. He vocalized his love for my kids and all the children at the school, regardless of ethnicity. The next day he took the flag off his vehicle. He too received liberation.

Here are some ways you can start speaking up and leading out.

Be on the lookout for opportunities. When you witness disparaging behaviors or actions of a friend, family member, or coworker, speak up. It's awkward, we know. But your speaking up to Uncle Bill at Thanksgiving could be the difference between Uncle Bill persisting in racism or abandoning racist practices. Are we suggesting a shouting match? No. You can be kind, humble, and firm at the same time. Your speaking up could also allow the people of color in his life, at the table, gatherings, or at work to feel seen and heard. When you speak up, know that you are creating an opportunity for more dialogue. You are blazing a trail toward a more inclusive environment.

Leverage your social media for good. In the wake of the racial violence of 2020, "Blackout Tuesday" was born. On that Tuesday, June 2, millions of social media users posted solid black images to their social feeds to show their solidarity with the Black community. It was a powerful statement. Individuals, businesses, churches, janitors, stay-at-home moms, and CEOs all participated. Though impressive, the show of solidarity and strength may never be witnessed again. So we must commit to keep the conversation going. When a racial incident happens, speak up and lead out. As a person of color, it always encourages me (Josh) to see my White brothers and sisters standing in solidarity with us. It strengthens my resolve when I read the posts of other people of color speaking out on things that matter. When we engage on social media, we make our position clear: *Racial justice matters to me. I stand for reconciliation.*

Speak out when it most counts. It can be easy for the majority to place the burden on people of color to call out racism. But in the work of reconciliation, *everyone* bears the burden. We need our White brothers and sisters to leverage their power, position, and privilege for the good of people of color. Too many times we've experienced a power dynamic or bore witness to racism, while our White counterparts remained silent, only to nod and affirm us afterward. Reconciler, we *need* you to speak up and lead out.

Commitment 2: Advocate with Compassion and Conviction

As believers, we have abundant opportunities to be advocates in all spheres of our society: we can be invested in government on the local, state, and national levels; we can be involved with colleges, schools, the marketplace, etc.; we can engage with organizations that specifically advocate on behalf of the marginalized, oppressed, and the disenfranchised. Above all, we advocate to support the flourishing of all image bearers.

As we observe laws and policies that disproportionately affect people of color—be it underfunding schools, poor policing for communities of color, harsher sentencing, weightier penalties for certain crimes, incentivizing the wealthy—we steward our power to seek change. Many of these policies are decided on the local and state levels.

Justin Giboney advocated this way. He founded City Roots ATL, located in Grove Park, a historically oppressed neighborhood in West Atlanta. In recent years, with the gentrification phenomenon, many upper-middle-class individuals and families have sought to buy real estate in the emerging part of the city, forcing many poorer families, most of whom are Black, out of the community for pennies on the dollar. City Roots ATL has sought to raise awareness about this issue through grassroots organizing, attending city council meetings, and making their voices heard.

Our fight for racial justice may not be as massive as bringing about the Civil Rights Act of 1964 or the 1971 landmark victory for women's rights. But every step we take in the right direction is progress.

Your advocacy need not be political in nature only. Perhaps you're a student on a college campus. You can use your influence and voice to make the campus a better place for minorities, women, or our disabled neighbors. Whatever your position, whatever your power, whatever your privilege, you can seize the opportunity to bring change and to support policies and practices that bring about justice for those marginalized or oppressed. Here are some other ways to begin advocating.

Connect with an existing group. Find a group, Christian or otherwise, that is advocating on behalf of marginalized people groups. Perhaps it's a group fighting for a fair wage for women, or advocating for affordable housing access, or accessible health care in poorer communities. Each step in the right direction is one foot closer to a complete victory.

Get to know the people who can help you in your pursuit. Do you know your chief of police? Local officials? School board members? State-level congresspeople? A better question is, do they know you? Have you pressed the issue or made your concerns known to them? Many would love to get to know their constituents and to serve their communities better. Reconciler, get to know them. Change comes when we must marry our values and our votes. Require civic leaders to represent the one to get the other.

Commitment 3: Pick a Justice Initiative and Serve Long-Term

One of the ways we can practice our faith differently and embody the values of God's kingdom is by picking a justice initiative and serving long-term. As Eugene Peterson wrote: "Repentance is a realization that what God wants from you and what you want from God are not going to be achieved by doing the same old things, thinking the same old thoughts."[2]

Jesus wants to use you to make things better. Pick an initiative and volunteer. Get invested in the details about the organization, about the injustice and alternative solutions. Give yourself to it.

No one embodies this value like Dan Crain. He is a reconciler who has given his life to seeing justice established in his community. Nearly a decade ago he and his family moved to historic South Atlanta, in one of the most distressed and racially oppressed neighborhoods. He didn't move there to be its savior. He moved there to be a member of the community, to build his family in the rich soil of a Black and Brown neighborhood. He moved there to be a voice and pillar for justice. He participates with several organizations that are doing good in the community. He voices his concerns to civic leaders. He advocates for good programming from other nonprofits that dignify and build the beloved community. He has chosen to situate his life so that he can serve the cause of racial justice long term.

God may not be calling you to serve justice in such a radical way as Dan does. But wherever He places you, invest in being radical in practice, participation, and commitment to the long term. What does that look like?

Move toward the tension. Our tendency is to fight, flight, or freeze in the face of conflict. Make it a principle in your life to stay and fight for what you believe in. Don't retreat. We have to stop outsourcing compassion and plant our feet and open our hands to serve. Pick an organization fighting for racial justice and do the following:

- Lend your strength. What expertise or skill do you have that could be of benefit?
- Lend your network. Who do you know that would be a good connection? Part of helping to meet a need may be using your network.
- Lend your voice. Socializing the good that these organizations are doing matters in a significant way. It raises awareness and builds social capital.
- Lend your prayers. Paul reminds us that we do not fight against flesh and blood, but against principalities in high places (see Eph. 6:12). Justice leaders need your prayers. Justice organizations need believers committed to interceding

on their behalf. Add your "amen" to what God is at work doing through these people and ministries.

TO LOVE MERCY . . .

Commitment 4: Give Generously

A dear friend by the name of Jack often reminds me (Josh) that justice grows in the womb of mercy. His point is that when Christians fall in love with mercy, the work of reconciliation, justice, repair, and restoration can begin to take place. We must become mercy-full, or better stated, full of mercy. One way to do that is by giving of our resources.

As Hazen and I have led OneRace, we have seen several tough seasons. In fact, there have been seasons in which one, or both of us, went unpaid for a time, while committing fifty-plus hours a week to the work of this movement. We do this because we see racial justice and reconciliation work as mission work. Reconciliation is indispensable to our discipleship practice. But justice work needs financial support. We could name twenty-five organizations that would benefit from your giving—organizations that are making a impact despite not having the support of a major institution backing them. They need your help.

Part of being a reconciler is to be a proponent of those doing good work, understanding that we can't do it all, but some can do what we can't. Some are called to host prayer gatherings, some are called to build relationship groups, others are called to equip. We are all invited to play a part. Sometimes that means supporting from the sidelines, knowing our generosity can go where we cannot. Paul spoke to this point: "If the willingness is there, the gift is acceptable according to what one has, not according to what one does not have" (2 Cor. 8:12 NIV).

> The world may not change, but you don't have to stay the same. Liberation starts from within.

Give. Then go beyond giving personally and leverage your personal, organizational, and social networks for financial capital for these organizations. We must make *funding* the work of racial justice as essential as our *doing* the work of racial justice. We must never forget money is an extension of the heart. As Jesus declared, "Where your treasure is, there your heart will be also" (Matt. 6:21).

Commitment 5: Intentionally Follow and Listen to Leaders of Color

I (Josh) recently realized that throughout my life, I have had zero bosses of color. Zero. Even in church, I have only attended congregations in which the lead pastor was White. This was a hard awakening. If a Black person has had this experience, what does that mean for our White siblings? Or Brown siblings?

I made the difficult choice to change churches—not that I was trying to segregate. I simply wanted to find a church in which the lead pastor was a person of color. From there I began to think about places I frequented, organizations I was a part of, and where I spent my money. Part of the journey for both people of color and White people is learning to love and affirm Black and Brown dignity. The world may not change, but you don't have to stay the same. Liberation starts from within.

In general in the Western world, White people don't have to follow people of color. People of color don't have to follow people of color either. In a world in which White culture and the White experience is deemed superior, we must intentionally dismantle this ideology. One of the best ways to do this is to listen to voices of color. Read, listen, shop, attend church, consume information about communities of color from people of color, and find a mentor who is a person of color. Go to spaces that challenge your view.

To get started, read such books as *Jesus and the Disinherited* by Howard Thurman, *Roadmap to Reconciliation* by Brenda Salter McNeil, *Unsettling Truths* by Mark Charles and Soong-Chan Rah, and *Oneness Embraced* by Tony Evans.

Listen to podcasts such as *Truth's Table, Diversity Gap, Pass the Mic, Chasing Justice,* and *Be the Bridge.*

Watch such movies and television specials as *The African Americans: Many Rivers to Cross, Thirteenth,* and PBS's *Asian Americans.*

We need to make intentional efforts to follow, submit to, and receive instruction from people of color. Authority and leadership are formative and can open our hearts to loving mercy. We stand to learn much from a diversity of voices and approaches to history, theology, and entertainment. If you find yourself dominated by singular approaches and voices, it may be time to change the rhythms of your life to dismantle cultural superiority.

> Ultimately our work as reconcilers is to become and see others become Christlike.

Commitment 6: Raise Up Reconcilers

One of our greatest joys is to be able to invest in those around us as Christlikeness is being formed in them. It is much the same with reconciliation. The more we can think of reconciliation as spiritual formation, the more it will have a treasured place in our hearts. Jesus loves reconciliation, so much so that He died for that very cause. As we become more equipped, we cannot hesitate to pass it on.

Part of our journey into mercy is that our hearts are filled with wanting to pass the knowledge and insight we have received to others in order to raise them up as reconcilers. As we pursue the calling of a reconciler, we have the apostle Paul's example as he intentionally discipled young Timothy: "What you have heard from me in the presence of many witnesses entrust to faithful men, who will be able to teach others also" (2 Tim. 2:2). Paul provides a clear framework for *how* we should invest into people and *why*. Because ultimately our work as reconcilers is to become and see others become Christlike.

Mrs. Karen Loritts invests in raising up reconcilers. Her passion for racial discipleship is both intentional and incidental—intentional in those she invests in on their journey toward Christlikeness, and incidental in those who receive words of encouragement, insight, and correction. For example, she has practiced intentional discipleship as she joins others on implementing several reconciliation initiatives in her church and community.

Those who recognize her leadership know she is for kingdom and justice. She builds it into every initiative she engages with. As for her incidental discipleship—she makes it a point to live these values out so that those she comes in contact with can't help but be impacted by these values. She models well what it means to make disciples.

TO WALK HUMBLY . . .

Commitment 7: Engage in a Radical Persistence in Prayer

Our work for reconciliation and change must begin in prayer and continue in prayer. We need to fall broken before the Lord, with a clear understanding that this world and individuals can't yield and sustain kingdom fruit apart from His intervention. We must admit our neediness. We need God to intervene in human history. While good fruit can emerge apart from God—this is the work of common grace—we too know that reformation of the church and society won't come apart from prayer. Though we covered much of this in the "own the story" chapters, it is worth reiterating, as reconcilers must live this value out.

Many forget that the civil rights movement was in fact a gospel movement—and one that centered on prayer. It was the power of God that gave Fannie Lou Hamer, a civil rights activist, the ability to stand for justice. It was the Holy Spirit who gave Prathia Hall, another civil rights activist, the "I have a dream" language and empowered her to deliver her "thus saith the Lord" to Dr. Martin Luther King. And it was the Lord who gave Rosa Parks, who played a pivotal role in the Montgomery bus boycott, the courage to remain seated. These folks took to their knees in prayer that the Lord would offer something of Himself to give them the courage to stand. The same God they leaned on waits for us to come to Him with our needs as well. If we are going to see reconciliation in our lives, churches, and communities, we need the courage to stand. We must be rooted and grounded by prayer.

Before racism is a statement, a law, a behavior, an idea, or an attitude, it is a principality (see Eph. 6:12). Prayer allows us to recognize racism's demonic influence. Radical, unfailing, unceasing prayer gives us the power and strength to overthrow it and to see real reformation come to the church and to America.

At the time of this writing, OneRace has hosted nearly one hundred public prayer gatherings with thousands of Christians in attendance. We acknowledge that if we don't center ourselves on the power and presence of Jesus, we will begin to wage war according to the flesh. As reconcilers, we must trust and believe

Jesus is at work reconciling all things to Himself. Thus, we partner with Him and the work He is doing in the world through prayer.

Commitment 8: Practice Cultural Humility

At the risk of sounding insensitive, we'd like to say that you are not the center of the universe (neither are we). Jesus is. Our efforts toward reconciliation are worthless if we do not lift up our Redeemer and Reconciler and seek His ways and His desires above all. We know from Scripture that one of His desires is that we would love our neighbors with the same fierce loyalty and commitment as we do ourselves. As we move forward in that kind of love to change the story, here are a few ways we can operate with cultural humility.

Hold space for people of color. We need to make room by getting out of the way. Whether it's in conversation, church, or at the workplace, we need to be aware of and give them space to offer their insights and wisdom. I (Josh) can't tell you how many times I've been in conversation with someone, particularly my White siblings, who, zealous as they may be, trample over me in conversation on things that are race related. It's as if they are saying, *I know best.* "Be quick to listen and slow to talk," the apostle James tells us (James 1:19). Make space in conversation, in your life, in organization, and in your community.

Forsake your preferences. Early in our journey together, Hazen and I had many rubs, points of tension, because of his insistence on things being his way. His inflexibility needed some deconstruction and some direct conflict. I needed to remind him about the biblical values we share. And he needed to humbly receive those reminders. Fortunately, we were able to cross that bridge and have had many heart and cultural conversations since then.

The temptation for many of us working in the race space is to develop a savior complex. To avoid moving into that arrogance, make it a value to amplify underrepresented voices. When we do the work of deconstructing our native culture, that opens the way for us to live according to a higher culture—kingdom culture. I (Josh) find myself practicing this idea as it relates to my sisters in Christ. Because men can tend to be know-it-alls, we mansplain and use the force of our presence to create an opening for us to express ourselves and push forward our preferences. This can create an uncomfortable power dynamic for women. So in the words of my wife, I learned I need to "dial down, ask lots of questions, and try not to assume." This makes a path for interaction and deep engagement.

Don't give up when you get it wrong. Undoubtedly, at times you will get it wrong. You will say the wrong thing. You will have some prejudices and cultural preferences that will impact your cross-cultural engagement. Embrace humility when it does. Practice humility before the Lord and with those you are connected to. Humility is the glue that will bind relationships together and will soothe hearts to lean more toward forgiveness.

Commitment 9: Stand Uncompromisingly on Who God Made Each of Us to Be

For people of color, we must decide to bring our full selves into every environment. *Every. One.* We need to choose not to fit neatly into the box of expectations that culture has placed on us. This will do a few things, which we can prepare for: (1) it will cause us to be displaced in the environment, allowing us to move on to a place that accepts who God has made us to be; (2) we become part of reforming the culture of said environment. This is all good, because it allows us to show up ready to participate in destroying the wall of hostility between people groups and to build bridges to new un-charted territory.

For White people and especially leaders, one of our most important roles is to be an encourager and advocate to our Black and Brown siblings when they take these steps. The simple truth is that we can make it harder or easier for people of color to bring their whole selves to our organizations and communities. As those frequently in the majority or in positions of power, we can influence things both big and small that can send positive or negative messages on whether people of color are going to be received. Let's follow Paul's insight and choose to "encourage one another and build one another up" (1 Thess. 5:11).

A simple example is in our Sunday morning expressions of worship. Churches can make decisions that deeply impact how people of color feel received in our pews. This is a great place to incorporate different cultures and styles to allow everyone to worship in a way that connects them with God the way He created them to. Imagine a congregational expression of worship with people of color empowered at *all* levels of leadership, with representation and authority. That would be growth! And consider a worship expression that has authority in leadership, representation, and freedom of expression—meaning we don't just play Christian contemporary music. We invest in getting musicians who can skillfully play gospel-style music, one of the most complex styles to master. We may need to teach our White members to engage in worship to a rhythm and sound that strikes them at first as very different from what they are used to. But if we are able to add C. C. Winans, Kirk Franklin, or Fred Hammond to our Sunday morning worship expressions, we might find that we will delight, amaze, and welcome people coming from traditional "Black church" backgrounds.

Representation is only one part of the equation of truly building a reconciled culture. We must understand that it takes representation, yes, but also real empowerment at all levels. If we welcome representation, authority, and expression into our boardrooms, classrooms, and sanctuaries, we will have the opportunity to discover the very best of what we have to offer one another. As Paul tells us in Philippians 2:4, "Let each of you look not only to his own interests, but also to the interests of others."

Commitment 10: Center Yourself on the Great Reconciler

Jesus is at work reconciling people to Himself and reconciling people to each other. Jesus must be the center of our efforts to change the story. He is the reason and motivation for our work, and so the impact of our engagement must reflect Him. It's important for us to never forget that *Christ* is doing the reconciling, we are but co-laborers with Him. And what a joy it is to partner with the great Reconciler as He reconciles all things to Himself: "In him all the fullness of God was pleased to dwell, and through him to reconcile to himself all things, whether on earth or in heaven, making peace by the blood of his cross" (Col. 1:19–20).

THE CHANGE IN ACTION

I'll never forget standing at the Georgia State Capitol at a press conference that Hazen and I were hosting in the summer of 2020. We were calling the church to stand up against the racial violence of the season and pray for reconciliation and justice. It was a powerful moment. On this same day we rolled out The OneRace Statement on Righteousness and Justice:

> We reject passive acceptance of social norms that create a
> permissive atmosphere for racial violence, and we refuse

to be silent and complicit with systemic racism and we call others in the body of Christ to act decisively. We all have varying degrees of power, position, and privilege, and in following the example of our Savior as described in Philippians 2, we must count others as more important than ourselves, and exercise our power, position, and privilege for the betterment of those not like us.

We didn't stop there. We used our voices and influence to call on our civic leaders, on both sides of the aisle, to come together to snuff out racist policies and practices in our day:

> For our civic leaders: We are calling on the law creators, law interpreters, and law enforcers in the state of Georgia to put fresh eyes on the current statutes, and to work to ensure that the laws are written and enforced in ways that are equitable toward all. When legislation and enforcement enable one segment of the population to feel safe and another segment of the population to feel endangered, changes are necessary. We are calling on our elected representatives to make such changes, and for law enforcement at every level to act expeditiously against racially motivated crimes.

We invited leaders in our city to sign it, share it, and live it as an act of solidarity and an affirmation of the truth.

It is time-out for strawman arguments, and past time for us to be faithful to the gospel mandate that beckons us toward reconciliation. If we are not cautious and faithful to the requirements of Scripture that commands us to do justice, love mercy, and walk humbly with God, and to love others as we love ourselves, we have great fear that we will live beneath our privilege and repeat the errors of the past.

But history doesn't have to repeat itself. And we have hope that the church is going to ensure it won't, by the grace and mighty hand of God working in and through us as reconcilers. We must get busy doing the work of the compassionate Samaritan.

Dr. John Perkins was right when he told us that "leadership is a calling." *You* have been called. And though the work is difficult, we believe you are up to the challenge and are ready to receive the blessings of living as a reconciler.

As you move forward in this journey, we offer this prayer for you and for the great work that lies ahead:

> *We pray, Father, make us one even as You and Jesus are one. Let us learn to love across color, class, and culture. Let the love we have for one another be a sign to the church and to the world that we are Your disciples. And let us evermore remain faithful to do justly, love mercy, and walk humbly with You, our Savior and our God. Amen.*

Notes

CHAPTER 1: ON EARTH AS IT IS IN HEAVEN

1. Charles Reagan Wilson, "The Religion of the Lost Cause: Ritual and Organization of the Southern Civil Religion, 1865–1920," *The Journal of Southern History*, vol. 46, no. 2, Southern Historical Association, 219–38, https://doi.org/10.2307/2208359.

2. Benjamin Powers, "In the Shadow of Stone Mountain," Smithsonian, May 4, 2018, https://www.smithsonianmag.com/history/shadow-stone-mountain-180968956/.

3. "Ku Klux Klan," Southern Poverty Law Center, accessed October 5, 2021, https://www.splcenter.org/fighting-hate/extremist-files/ideology/ku-klux-klan.

4. Jemar Tisby, *Color of Compromise: The Truth about the American Church's Complicity in Racism* (Grand Rapids, MI: Zondervan, 2020), 71.

5. Kelly J. Baker, *Gospel According to the Klan: The KKK's Appeal to Protestant Americans, 1915–1930* (Lawrence, KS: University Press of Kansas, 2017, 5–6. Emphasis in the original.

6. W. E. B. Du Bois, *The Souls of Black Folk* (Chicago: A. C. McClurg & Co., 1907), 2.

7. Juliana Kaplan and Madison Hoff, "These Two Charts Show How the Racial Wealth Gap Has Gotten Even Wider Over the Years," *Business Insider*, March 24, 2021, https://www.businessinsider.com/charts-how-much-wealth-each-race-ethnicity-held-2020-2021-3.

8. Poverty Facts, "The Population of Poverty USA," accessed October 5, 2021, https://www.povertyusa.org/facts.

9. John Gramlich, "The Gap Between the Number of Blacks and Whites in Prison Is Shrinking," Pew Research Center, April 30, 2019, https://www.pewresearch.org/fact-tank/2019/04/30/shrinking-gap-between-number-of-blacks-and-whites-in-prison/.

10. "Mapping Police Violence," accessed October 5, 2021, https://mapping policeviolence.org/.

11. Ryan Nunn, Jana Parsons, and Jay Shambaugh, "Race and Underemployment in the US Labor Market," Brookings, August 1, 2019, https://www.brookings.edu/blog/up-front/2019/08/01/race-and-underemployment-in-the-u-s-labor-market/. Note that these numbers are from 2019. The COVID-19 pandemic created unemployment numbers much greater.

12. Robin Bleiweis, "Quick Facts about the Gender Wage Gap," Center for American Progress, March 24, 2020, https://www.americanprogress.org/issues/women/reports/2020/03/24/482141/quick-facts-gender-wage-gap/.

13. Barna Group and The Reimagine Group, *Where Do We Go from Here?* (Ventura, CA: Barna, 2019), 45–53.

14. Ibid.

15. Klyne Snodgrass, *Ephesians: NIV Application Commentary* (Grand Rapids, MI: Zondervan Academic, 1996), 93–156.

16. Ibid.

17. Ibid.

CHAPTER 2: JOURNEYING TOWARD WELLNESS

1. Martin Luther King, Jr., *Where Do We Go from Here?: Community or Chaos* (Boston: Beacon Press, 2010), 33.

2. Latasha Morrison, *Be the Bridge: Pursuing God's Heart for Reconciliation* (Colorado Springs, CO: WaterBrook, 2019), 33.

3. Ray Vander Laan, *In the Dust of the Rabbi Discovery Guide* (Grand Rapids, MI: Zondervan, 2006), 193.

4. Schaff's New Testament Commentary, StudyLight.org, accessed October 8, 2021, https://www.studylight.org/commentaries/eng/scn/john-17.html.

CHAPTER 3: *KNOW* THE STORY OF RACISM IN AMERICA

1. Yuliya Parshina-Kottas, Anjali Singhvi, and Audra D. S. Burch, "What the 1921 Tulsa Race Massacre Destroyed," *New York Times*, May 24, 2021, https://www.nytimes.com/interactive/2021/05/24/us/tulsa-race-massacre.html.

2. "'Dad' Clark, Oldest Known Race Riot Survivor, Dies," News On 6, May 22, 2012, http://www.newson6.com/story/5e364d2e2f69d76f62065422/dad-clark-oldest-known-tulsa-race-riot-survivor-dies.

3. Martin Luther King, Jr., "Dr. Martin Luther King, Jr.'s Visit to WMU," December 18, 1963, Western Michigan University Library, https://libguides.wmich.edu/mlkatwmu/speech.

4. Though we don't have the space in this book to explore race in-depth, we offer a cursory overview to give you a taste. Here we focus primarily on the experience of Black and White people in America, merely highlighting our Indigenous, Hispanic, and Asian neighbors. This approach is not to downplay others' experiences, but to focus on the groups that have had the greatest impact on shaping American culture and race relations. That said, we encourage you not to stop your education with this book, but to pursue other historical sources for more understanding, engagement, and exploration.

5. "The Trans-Atlantic Slave Trade," Lowcountry Digital History Initiative, accessed October 6, 2021, https://ldhi.library.cofc.edu/exhibits/show/africanpassageslowcountryadapt/introductionatlanticworld/trans_atlantic_slave_trade.

6. Slavery actually arrived in America in 1565 under Spanish-held St. Augustine. Jamestown played a more significant role because it served as a beginning stage for what would become the institution of slavery in America. Olivia B. Waxman, "The First Africans in Virginia Landed in 1619. It Was a Turning Point for Slavery in American History—But Not the Beginning," *Time*, August 20, 2019, https://time.com/5653369/august-1619-jamestown-history/.

7. "The First Africans," Jamestown Rediscovery, accessed October 6, 2021, https://historicjamestowne.org/history/the-first-africans/.

8. J. Gordon Hylton, "When Did Slavery Really End in the United States?", *Marquette University Law School Faculty* blog, January 15, 2013, https://

law.marquette.edu/facultyblog/2013/01/when-did-slavery-really-end-in-the-united-states/comment-page-1/.

9. "Trans-Atlantic Slave Trade—Estimates," Slave Voyages, accessed October 8, 2021, https://www.slavevoyages.org/assessment/estimates.

10. Brendan Wolfe, "Slave Ships and the Middle Passage," Encyclopedia Virginia, February 1, 2021, https://encyclopediavirginia.org/entries/slave-ships-and-the-middle-passage.

11. Deborah B. Berry and Kelly B. French, "Slavery, Black History, DNA Genealogy," *USA Today*, August 21, 2019, https://www.usatoday.com/in-depth/news/nation/2019/08/21/wanda-tucker-angola-slavery-1619-history-america-black-family/2016591001/.

12. Robin Sidel, "A Historian's Quest Links J. P. Morgan to Slave Ownership," May 10, 2005, https://www.wsj.com/articles/SB111568595843228824.

13. Stephen Smith and Kate Ellis, "Shackled Legacy," APM Reports, September 4, 2017, https://www.apmreports.org/episode/2017/09/04/shackled-legacy.

14. Associated Press, "Aetna Apologizes for Slave Insurance," *Los Angeles Times*, March 11, 2000, https://www.latimes.com/archives/la-xpm-2000-mar-11-fi-7637-story.html.

15. Ta-Nehisi Coates, "Slavery Made America," *The Atlantic*, June 24, 2014, https://www.theatlantic.com/business/archive/2014/06/slavery-made-america/373288/.

16. Rick Hampson, "How an Accidental Encounter Brought Slavery to the United States," *USA Today*, December 16, 2019, https://www.usatoday.com/in-depth/news/nation/2019/08/21/american-slavery-began-1619-project-documents-brutal-journey/1968793001/.

17. David Blight, *Frederick Douglass: Prophet of Freedom* (New York: Simon & Schuster, 2018), 35–47.

18. Frederick Douglass, *Narrative of the Life of Frederick Douglass*, The University of Virginia, 1845, http://utc.iath.virginia.edu/abolitn/abaufda14t.html.

19. David Blight, *Frederick Douglass*, 35–47.

20. Frederick Douglass, as quoted in "(1841) Frederick Douglass, 'The Church and Prejudice,'" BlackPast, March 15, 2012, https://www.blackpast.org/african-american-history/1841-frederick-douglass-church-and-prejudice/.

21. Frederick Douglass, "Letter to Thomas Auld (September 3, 1848)," Yale MacMillan Center, https://glc.yale.edu/letter-thomas-auld-september-3-1848.

22. Elizabeth Prine Pauls, "Native American," *Encyclopedia Britannica*, August 17, 2021, https://www.britannica.com/topic/Native-American.

23. Russell Thornton, *American Indian Holocaust and Survival: A Population History since 1492* (Norman, OK: University of Oklahoma Press, 1987), 43.

24. Samuel Carter III, *Cherokee Sunset: A Nation Betrayed: A Narrative of Travail and Triumph, Persecution and Exile* (New York: Doubleday, 1976), 232.

25. "Indian Removal Act," *Encyclopedia Britannica*, November 13, 2019, https://www.britannica.com/topic/Indian-Removal-Act.

26. Elizabeth Prine Pauls, "Trail of Tears," *Encyclopedia Britannica*, November 11, 2019, https://www.britannica.com/event/Trail-of-Tears.

27. Abraham Lincoln, "Transcript of the Proclamation," January 1, 1863, National Archives, https://www.archives.gov/exhibits/featured-documents/emancipation-proclamation/transcript.html.

28. History.com Editors, "Black Leaders During Reconstruction," History.com, January 26, 2021, https://www.history.com/topics/american-civil-war/black-leaders-during-reconstruction.

29. "Lynching in America: Confronting the Legacy of Racial Terror," Equal Justice Initiative, accessed October 9, 2021, https://eji.org/reports/lynching-in-america/.

30. "Mary Turner, Pregnant, Lynched in Georgia for Publicly Criticizing Husband's Lynching," Equal Justice Initiative, accessed October 9, 2021, https://calendar.eji.org/racial-injustice/may/19.

31. Euell Nielsen, "Mary Turner (1899–1918)," Black Past, September 22, 2015, https://www.blackpast.org/african-american-history/mary-turner-1899-1918/.

32. "The Story of Mary Turner and the Lynching Rampage of 1918," Mary Turner Project, accessed October 6, 2021, https://www.maryturner.org.

33. Arlisha Norwood, "Ida B. Wells-Barnett," National Women's History Museum, 2017, https://www.womenshistory.org/education-resources/biographies/ida-b-wells-barnett.

34. Ida B. Wells, "Lynching Our National Crime," address at the National Negro Conference, June 1, 1909, Iowa State University, Archives of Women's Political Communication, https://awpc.cattcenter.iastate.edu/2017/03/09/mob-murder-in-a-christian-nation-june-1-1909/.

35. Frederick Douglass, as quoted in Ida B. Wells, *Southern Horrors: Lynch Law in All Its Phases*, 1892, Digital History, accessed October 9, 2021, https://www.digitalhistory.uh.edu/disp_textbook.cfm?smtID=3&psid=3614.

36. "Ida B. Wells-Barnett," Iowa State University, Archives of Women's Political Communication, accessed October 6, 2021, https://awpc.cattcenter.iastate.edu/directory/ida-b-wells/.

37. "Who Was Ella Baker," Ella Baker Center for Human Rights, https://ellabakercenter.org/who-was-ella-baker/.

38. Vicki L. Crawford, Jacqueline A. Rouse, Barbara Woods, et al., *Women in the Civil Rights Movement: Trailblazers and Torchbearers* (Bloomington, IN: Indiana University Press, 1990), 52–54.

39. Ibid., 52.

CHAPTER 4: *KNOW* THE STORY OF THE CHURCH

1. A Group of Clergy Men, "Letter to Dr. Martin Luther King," April 12, 1963, Teaching American History, https://teachingamericanhistory.org/library/document/letter-to-martin-luther-king/.

2. "Four Little Girls," National Park Service, accessed November 10, 2021, https://www.nps.gov/articles/fourlittlegirls.htm.

3. "(1963) George Wallace, Segregation Now, Segregation Forever," BlackPast, January 22, 2013, https://www.blackpast.org/african-american-history/speeches-african-american-history/1963-george-wallace-segregation-now-segregation-forever/.

4. "Vivian Juanita Malone Jones (1942–2005)," BlackPast, October 29, 2020, https://www.blackpast.org/african-american-history/vivian-juanita-malone-jones-1942-2005/.

5. Martin Luther King, Jr., "Letter from a Birmingham Jail," April 16, 1963, African Studies Center—University of Pennsylvania, https://www.africa.upenn.edu/Articles_Gen/Letter_Birmingham.html.

6. Frederick Douglass, *Narrative of the Life of Frederick Douglass,* The University of Virginia, 1845, http://utc.iath.virginia.edu/abolitn/abaufda14t .html.

7. Stephen Le Feuvre, "The Curse of Ham: Getting It Horribly Wrong," The Gospel Coalition, March 3, 2020, https://africa.thegospelcoalition. org/article/curse-of-ham/; Garrett Kell, "Damn the Curse of Ham: How Genesis 9 Got Twisted into Racist Propaganda," Gospel Coalition, January 9, 2021, https://www.thegospelcoalition.org/article/damn-curse-ham/.

8. Garrett Kell, "Damn the Curse."

9. Michael Emerson and Christian Smith, *Divided by Faith* (New York: Oxford University Press, 2001), 34.

10. Ibid., 26.

11. Ibid.

12. Jemar Tisby, *Color of Compromise: The Truth about the American Church's Complicity in Racism* (Grand Rapids, MI: Zondervan, 2020), 47.

13. George Whitefield, *The Works of the Rev. George Whitefield, M.A.* (London: Edward and Charles Dilly, 1771), 32.

14. Emerson and Smith, *Divided by Faith,* 26–27.

15. Ibid.

16. Ibid.

17. Ibid., 32.

18. Kate Shellnutt, "What Is Billy Graham's Friendship with Martin Luther King Jr. Worth?," *Christianity Today,* February 23, 2018, https://www .christianitytoday.com/news/2018/february/billy-graham-martin- luther-king-jr-friendship-civil-rights.html.

19. Kristin Butler, "A Tale of Two Preachers," PBS, May 12, 2021, https:// www.pbs.org/wgbh/americanexperience/features/billy-graham-tale- two-preachers/.

20. Martin Luther King, Jr., "To Billy Graham," July 23, 1958, https:// kinginstitute.stanford.edu/king-papers/documents/billy-graham-0.

21. Grady Wilson, July 28, 1958, The Martin Luther King, Jr. Research and Education Institute—Stanford, https://kinginstitute.stanford.edu/king- papers/documents/grady-wilson.

22. Butler, "Tale of Two Preachers."

23. Ibid.

24. Ibid.

25. Ibid.

26. Pricilla Pope-Levison, "Richard Allen [Pennsylvania] (1760–1831)," BlackPast, October 18, 2007, https://www.blackpast.org/african-american-history/allen-richard-pennsylvania-1760-1831/.

27. "The Reverend Absalom Jones, 1746–1818," Episcopal Archives, accessed October 14, 2021, https://episcopalarchives.org/church-awakens/exhibits/show/leadership/clergy/jones.

28. Tisby, *Color of Compromise*, 53.

29. Pope-Levison, "Richard Allen."

30. Annette Gordon-Reed, "The Art of Persuasion: Harriet Beecher Stowe's 'Uncle Tom's Cabin,'" *The New Yorker*, June 13, 2011, https://www.newyorker.com/magazine/2011/06/13/the-persuader-annette-gordon-reed.

31. Ibid.

32. Ibid.

CHAPTER 6: *OWN* THE STORY THROUGH PERSONAL PRACTICES

1. Anthony Thompson, from a personal conversation.

CHAPTER 8: *OWN* THE STORY THROUGH CULTURAL HUMILITY

1. Timothy Keller, *Galatians for You: For Reading, for Feeding, for Leading* (Epsom, Surrey, England: Good Book, 2013).

2. Yehudah Mirsky, "Three Blessings," Jewish Ideas Daily, March 23, 2011, http://www.jewishideasdaily.com/848/features/three-blessings/.

3. Scot McKnight, *Galatians: The NIV Application Commentary* (Grand Rapids, MI: Zondervan).

4. Ibid.

5. Tony Evans, *Oneness Embraced: Reconciliation, the Kingdom, and How We Are Stronger Together* (Chicago: Moody, 2015), 89.

6. Rasool Berry, "Critical [G]race Theory: The Promise and Perils of CRT," Power to Change, February 16, 2021, https://p2c.com/students/articles/critical-grace-theory-the-promise-and-perils-of-crt/.

7. Evans, *Oneness Embraced*, 89–90.

8. Merriam Webster Dictionary, "Culture," accessed October 12, 2021, https://www.merriam-webster.com/dictionary/culture.

9. Soong-Chan Rah, *Many Colors: Cultural Intelligence for a Changing Church* (Chicago: Moody, 2010), 38.

10. Howard Thurman, *Jesus and the Disinherited* (Boston: Beacon Press, 1976), 5.

CHAPTER 9: *CHANGE* THE STORY

1. Martin Luther King, Jr., *Strength to Love* (Boston: Beacon Press, 1963), 59.

2. Martin Luther King, Jr., "Draft of Chapter VI, 'A Knock at Midnight,'" July 1, 1962 to March 31, 1963, The Martin Luther King, Jr. Research and Education Institute—Stanford University, https://kinginstitute.stanford.edu/king-papers/documents/draft-chapter-vi-knock-midnight.

3. John M. Perkins, *Dream with Me: Race, Love, and the Struggle We Must Win* (Grand Rapids, MI: Baker, 2017), 110.

4. Martin Luther King, Jr., *Stride toward Freedom: The Montgomery Story* (Boston: Beacon Press, 1958), 39.

5. Perkins, *Dream with Me*, 206.

6. LaTonya Gates, as quoted in Keri Janton, "PAWKids Founder Rises Above Past to Serve Community," *Atlanta Journal-Constitution*, July 6, 2021, https://www.ajc.com/inspire/pawkids-founder-rises-above-past-to-serve-community/R56LAHIHR5FKNPETKOCJCUQLK4/.

7. Ibid.

8. Martin Luther King, Jr., "Beyond Vietnam: A Time to Break Silence," sermon given at Riverside Church, New York City, April 4, 1967, Civil Rights Movement Archives, https://www.crmvet.org/info/mlk_viet.pdf.

CHAPTER 10: TEN COMMITMENTS OF A RECONCILER

1. Martin Luther King, Jr., "Letter from a Birmingham Jail," April 16, 1963, African Studies Center—University of Pennsylvania, https://www.africa.upenn.edu/Articles_Gen/Letter_Birmingham.html.

2. Eugene Peterson, *A Long Obedience in the Same Direction* (Downers Grove, IL: InterVarsity, 2019), 24.

About the Authors

JOSH CLEMONS is privileged to serve as the executive director and vice chairman for OneRace Movement. He has built a reputation as a lover of God, builder of people, and a reconciler of cultures. Serving as an author and professor, and leading a racial reconciliation movement, Josh shares his insight, wisdom, and practical instruction, impacting audiences in both religious and secular communities. Josh is currently pursuing his Ph.D. at Fuller Theological Seminary. He resides in Atlanta, Georgia, with his wife, Lakisha, and two sons, Langston Grant and Duke Ellington.

HAZEN STEVENS is a founding member of OneRace Movement and currently serves as the executive pastor at GateCity Church in Lawrenceville, Georgia. Hazen has a passion for prayer and missions, and for thirteen years has served on staff with a 24/7 house of prayer, as the domestic director of a pioneer missions organization, and most recently as a pastor. He is married to his best friend, Hannah, and they reside with their four delightful children, Amarin, Chesed, Pearl, and Elisha, in metro-Atlanta where he was born and raised.

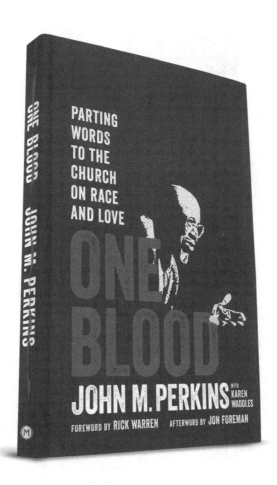

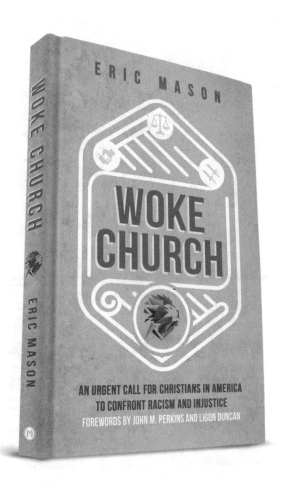